20th Century Costume Jewelry

1900 – 1980

IDENTIFICATION & VALUE GUIDE

RONNA LEE AIKINS

COLLECTOR BOOKS

A Division of Schroeder Publishing Co., Inc.

Front cover, left to right: Necklace of "poor man's jade," commonly known as Peking glass. $130.00 – 180.00. See page 192; Graduated Omega style chain and clips. $110.00 – 150.00. See page 62; Sunflower stretch pin. $10.00 – 20.00. See page 51; Rhinestones necklace. $90.00 – 180.00. See page 135; Christmas tree pin. $50.00 – 100.00. See page 179; Brilliant blue glass necklace. $180.00 – 230.00. See page 199; Antique gold leaf pin. $60.00 – 90.00. See page 140; Topaz and aqua brooch. $115.00 – 145.00. See page 140; Demi-parure silver-tone clip earrings and brooch. $105.00 – 135.00. See page 95; Rainbow crystal necklace $200.00 – 280.00. See page 30; Winter white plastic bracelet. $90.00 – 120.00. See page 207.

Back cover, left to right: 2½" Brooch. $125.00 – 155.00. See page 199; Silver beaded square bracelet. $110.00 – 150.00. See page 100; Cabochon center necklace. $170.00 – 220.00. See page 89; Brooch and clip earrings set. $130.00 – 170.00. See page 140; Wreath pin. $50.00 – 100.00. See page 179; Single strand, glass barrel bead necklace. $180.00 – 230.00. See page 191; Four strand necklace. $120.00 – 170.00. See page 43; Brooch and earrings. $135.00 – 165.00. See page 94.

Cover design by Beth Summers
Book design by Heather Warren
Cover photography by Charles R. Lynch

COLLECTOR BOOKS
P.O. Box 3009
Paducah, Kentucky 42002-3009

www.collectorbooks.com

Copyright © 2005 Ronna Lee Aikins

The current values in this book should be used only as a guide. They are not intended to set prices, which vary from one section of the country to another. Auction prices as well as dealer prices vary greatly and are affected by condition as well as demand. Neither the author nor the publisher assumes responsibility for any losses that might be incurred as a result of consulting this guide.

Searching For A Publisher?

We are always looking for people knowledgeable within their fields. If you feel that there is a real need for a book on your collectible subject and have a large comprehensive collection, contact Collector Books.

Contents

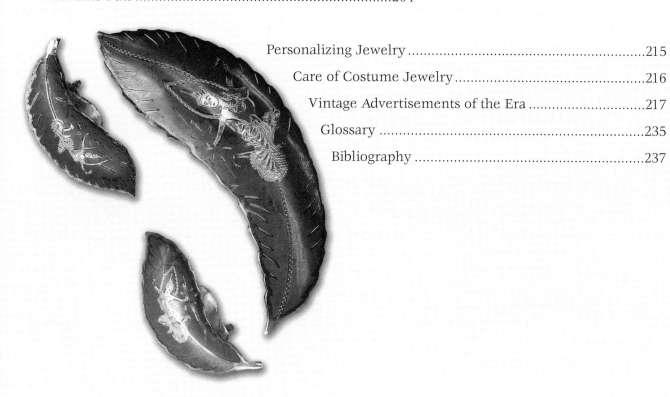

Dedication

This book is for Mrs. Nancy Aikins, whose initials stand for "natural accomplishments." We have all heard the saying, "finders keepers," which is not true in this case. As you may remember in the book *Brilliant Rhinestones*, I shared many of the pieces she gave to me. Mrs. Aikins is a finder of fantastic jewelry. On her many excursions of endless miles searching and knowing all of the right places to shop, she constantly is successful in seeking out more perfect pieces. Thank you, Nancy Aikins, for all of the grand, gracious, flashy, fun, and unique pieces that you have given me over the years.

Acknowledgments

Gail Ashburn, Amy Sullivan, and Beth Summers at Collector Books have been very kind and patient with me. They are so cooperative and easygoing. I also thank Collector Books for giving me an opportunity to not only enjoy a great hobby, but to document it and to share it with others.

Thanks to Whitey Aikins, my husband. This year was a real challenge; I really don't know how you fit the photography in your schedule, but I sincerely thank you.

To Abbey Little, my niece, who is becoming interested in her aunt's jewelry collection. I think Abbey has quite the eye. At age eight, she has her pick of great pieces.

To Rob Barkley, the treeologist, and to Mrs. Karla Barkley, who helped in the flower identification process, a special thanks.

Thanks to Uncle Mike Ault and Aunt Vonnie Tisa for a variety of reasons.

Thank you to my mother for the use of some of her jewelry.

Thanks to my friend Dave Overdorff.

Thanks to Quinn Little, my nephew, for all of his help packing jewelry.

Thanks to Denise's Antique Mall, Indiana, Pennsylvania, and Mary Grace.

Thanks to Gary and Bari Stuchal for sharing the Hobe set of Barris.

Note from the Author

I want to thank each of you who purchased my first book, *Brilliant Rhinestones*. I was elated to be surrounded by so many like minded people who have a passion for vintage jewelry. Since we all thirst for more information on pieces of jewelry, this book, my second, will have a much larger variety of styles and types of jewelry. I want to cover a broader scope for any of the adoring collectors that may have missed the selections in my first book.

Values and prices reflected in this book are determined from the jewelrys' selling prices in the co-ops, antique shops, antique shows, flea markets, and auctions. Prices differ geographically. The price is also based on condition, quality, documentation, and designer of the piece.

Please feel free to visit my website at www.ronnas-antiques.com

About the Author

Ronna Lee Aikins authored the book *Brilliant Rhinestones* in 2003. She has been interviewed on national radio and had articles about her book, with photos of her jewelry, featured in a national magazine. A costume jewelry collector for over 17 years, this book is based on Ronna Lee's accumulation. Ronna Lee also owned a unique boutique that offered vintage costume jewelry and contemporary clothing; she arranged fashion shows through her boutique. In Nashville, Tennessee, an upscale clothing store sold pieces of Ronna's jewelry collection. Her website, www.ronnas-antiques.com, now sells pieces of her jewelry collection. Ronna is involved with select antique shows and assists with antique organizations. She resides in Blairsville, Pennsylvania.

With special contributions by Katie Aikins:

Katie attended Bethany College and will be attending Seton Hill University in the fall of 2004. She helped her mother with shopping, writing, typing, and editing this book. Without Katie, it would have been impossible.

Ronna Lee Aikins

Katie Aikins

Periods of Times, Styles, and Manufacturers

Art Nouveau 1890 – 1910 Jewelry designs are flowing, spiral, wavy, floral patterns, and a hint of nature. At this time, America is the leading industrial nation in the world. Women play the stock market and become involved in business. The bicycle becomes popular; transportation is now the automobile that only the wealthy can afford. Dancing is in vogue; records sell at a brisk pace. Jewelry is produced in America, Bohemia, Denmark, England, France, Germany, and Italy.

Art Deco 1910 – 1930 People are interested in the Egyptian designs, American Indians, Russian ballet, and the Paris Exposition. Stones such as lapis lazuli and cornelian are popular. Emeralds, rubies, marcasites, ivory, and Bakelite are popular for jewelry designs. In November of 1920, KDKA starts broadcasting. New magazines are being published; movies are a part of Americans' lives. The stock market soars until the great crash in 1929. Uncertain what the thirties may bring, America enters the 1950s in a very turbulent manner. Jewelry is produced in America, Bohemia, Denmark, England, France, Germany, Italy, Israel, Mexico, and South America.

In the 1920s and the 1930s, pieces marked "TFK" are produced by Trifari. The exquisite workmanship of Trifari is imitative of fine jewelry. In the 1930s and the 1940s, Trifari produces a hefty amount of rhodium-plated pieces with a fine finish. They also produce "jelly bellies," usually animal motifs whose bodies are composed of Lucite. Trifari is known for the classic crown brooch, set with cabochon stones in varied colors.

Miriam Haskell is known for a very soft design style. The pieces are hand done from beads, pearls, gilt brass, and more. In the 1930s and the 1940s, the look is beads and seed pearls. Haskell's jewelry is not signed until the end of the 1940s and the early 1950s. The Haskell company develops the antique gold finish. Miriam Haskell is active until she retires in 1950, and sells the company to her younger brother, Joe Haskell. She dies at age 82 in 1981.

In the 1930s and the 1940s, Eisenberg's jewelry is marked Eisenberg original. This company is noted for using big, bold, beautiful Austrian crystals with a great design. During the war years, many designs are in sterling and attached to or used on clothing pieces; many are made for Nordstrom's. At Christmas time, Nordstrom's is known to carry the Eisenberg Ice, consisting of top grade stones from Swarovski.

Hobé is a family of jewelers with a great history dating back 200 years. They know their customer, the woman. They want a look of antique jewelry that is affordable. From the 1930s through the 1940s, they use wonderful faceted glass stones with enamel work. In 1940, a series of floral motifs is done in sterling. Carved ivory and cinnabar are part of the Hobé design.

Art Moderne 1935 – 1945 Jewelry is now creative in design, losing the Nouveau style. Pieces can be brilliant to dainty looking. Three-D is *en vogue*. Examples of metals used in jewelry are chrome and rhodium. Women now wear designs from the Orient. Hair is worn pulled up so women can showcase their decorative earrings and necklaces. Wars are discussed. On December 7, 1941, Pearl Harbor is bombed by the Japanese, and the United States becomes involved in World War II. In 1943, a 4-4 program takes hold where teenagers can work four hours and attend school four hours per day. The war creates shortages in everything from sugar to gasoline. Americans use ration coupons. On August 14, 1945, the war ends; America celebrates everywhere with church bells ringing in communities and cities, whistles blowing, and of course, the famous kiss of the nurse and the military man. Jewelry is produced in America, Bohemia, Denmark, England, France, Germany, Italy, Israel, Mexico, and South America.

Coro, in 1946, is the largest producer of costume jewelry in America. Over 2,000 different designs are in Coro's line. Every woman can afford Coro. In 1950, a line is produced under the name Vendome.

Modern 1950s bring gold-filled, sterling, and metals used in jewelry. Due to the shortages of goods from the war, retailers and manufacturers use items that they have in inventory. Slacks and culottes are worn. In 1956, "short shorts" become the rage! Then follows the ever popular chemise. It is accessorized with costume jewelry, gloves, furs, and hats. Jewelry items include heavy beads, bibs, bracelets, and long earrings that caress the shoulder.

Fun Facts About Jewelry

1896   The whistle bracelet is worn by women for protection while biking. The whistle has a two mile radius in which it can be heard.

1890 – 1920   Amber, known in Greek as "Lectron," is popular. Celluloid is now in style. It gives an expensive look.

1909   Screw-back earrings are introduced. Bracelets are worn on bare arms or over the sleeves.

1920   Pearls are the most popular necklace; a must have for any wardrobe!

1925   Long, roped beads, dangling earrings, bracelets, crystals, and rhinestones are fashionable. Birthstones are quite popular, and synthetic stones are now becoming highly advertised. Fine, faceted beads such as jet, and crystal are en vogue. Belt buckles and shoe clips with rhinestones are worn.

1920 – 1930   Bakelite, a new plastic invented by Leo Hendrick Baekeland, is popular.

1933   The November 11 issue of *Collier's* magazine states that massiveness is important in jewelry. Dress, hat, fur, and handbag clips are in style.

1935   Scottie dog pins are popular and stylish.

1946   Providence, Rhode Island, is declared costume jewelry capital of the United States.

1947   Western wear clothing by Marge Riley is *en vogue*.

1950s   Beaded sweaters, sweater clips, rhinestones, and matching accessories are the look.

1953   Aurora borealis is new, and shoppers are drawn to the look.

1960s   Jackie O. sets a jewelry fashion statement by wearing stylish costume jewelry and clothing that are copied by women in many countries. Charm bracelets are the "it" pieces.

1970s   Women enter the workplace and are wearing real gold. Gold chains are everywhere.

1980s   These are glamorous years with the shows *Dallas*, *Dynasty*, and *Knots Landing*. The Reagans are in the White House. Barbara Bush is known for her pearls.

1990s   Women are educated about the old jewelry their grandmothers wore. They want to have the nostalgia, along with the art form, of jewelry. Interest in the "vintage market" accelerates.

December 15, 2003   When asked by Diane Sawyer what he is getting Laura for Christmas, President George W. Bush's amazing response is "fake jewelry."

Birthstones and Flowers

Months	Stones (Meaning)	Flowers
January	Garnet (constancy)	Carnation, Snowdrop
February	Amethyst (sincerity)	Violet, Primrose
March	Aquamarine, Bloodstone (courage)	Jonquil, Daffodil
April	Diamond (innocence)	Sweet Pea, Daisy
May	Emerald (love, success)	Lily of the Valley, Hawthorn
June	Pearl, Moonstone, Alexandrite (health, longevity)	Rose, Honeysuckle
July	Ruby (contentment)	Larkspur, Waterlily
August	Peridot, Sardonyx (married happiness)	Poppy, Gladiolus
September	Sapphire (clear thinking)	Aster, Morning Glory
October	Opal, Tourmaline (hope)	Calendula, Cosmos
November	Topaz (fidelity)	Chrysanthemum
December	Turquoise, Zircon (prosperity)	Narcissus, Holly

Adorning Accessories

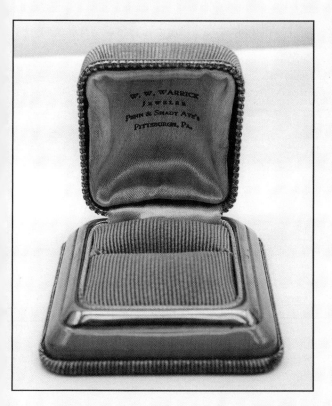

Rocking ring box. Inscribed "W.W WARRICK JEWELER, Penn & Shady Ave's, Pittsburgh, PA." From the 1940s. $15.00 – 20.00.

The original paper tag on the mirror reads, "made in Italy." The original powder puff is still in place. A very nice picture on the front of this heavy compact. 1940s. $80.00 – 120.00.

Beautiful, bold sunglasses. These black, round frames have rhinestones in the center division and near the hinges. From the late 1950s. $20.00 – 40.00.

Mother-of-pearl square compact. Gold leaves in sand are mixed with pink, blue, and off-white seashells to make a robust flower. The flower is complemented by a blue bow; butterflies add beauty to this piece. Late 1940s to the early 1950s. $75.00 – 105.00.

This outrageously beautiful compact has a white plastic top sprinkled with faux pearls. 1950s. Unsigned. $65.00 – 95.00.

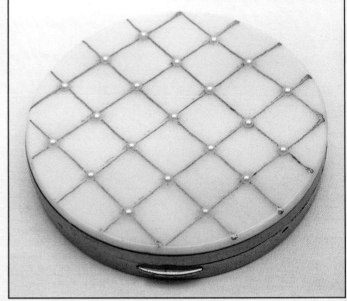

Made by Volupte U.S.A. This square compact is done in gold tone and has a design of a variety of colors in a safari scene. Hints of India. 1940s. $75.00 – 115.00.

Brilliant butterflies. Gold-tone base encompasses the butterfly painting signed by artist Holmes Grey; with its original box, signed "Stratton, England." Late 1940s to the mid-1950s. $85.00 – 125.00.

A smoking cigarette case. Mother-of-pearl plating. 25 squares make up this pastel pretty. Unsigned. Mid-1940s to the late 1950s. $80.00 – 120.00.

Silver-tone cigarette case with a rhinestone top. Rhinestones are glued in shallow cups. Unsigned. 1940s to the 1950s. $80.00 – 125.00.

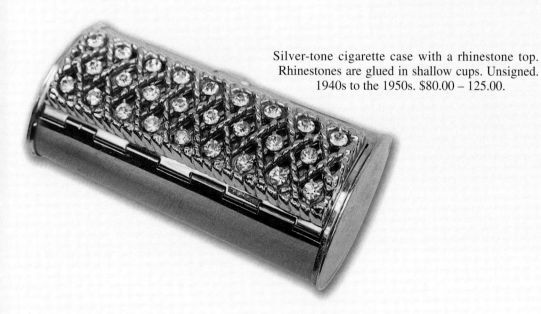

Daring dress clips have two rows of rhine[stones set in nice oval shapes. 2¼". 1940[s]. Unsigned. $120.00 – 150.00.

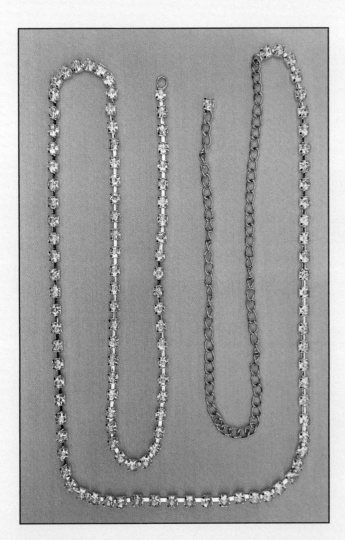

(Surrounding) White, plastic, flower hair pins with gold-tone sternums that hold a single rhinestone. These are typically used in buns. Unsigned. 1950s. $40.00 – 80.00. (Center) White, plastic feathers with three flowers surrounding. In the centers of the flowers are single rhinestones. Unsigned. 1950s. $10.00 – 30.00.

Bombastic belt measures 28¼". From the late 1950s. Very flashy! The adjustable chain measures 10¼". Unsigned. $100.00 – 140.00.

(Left) This creative compact has a nicely engraved silver-tone top. A square is there for initials, but no initials are engraved in the square. Holds the original powder. 2¼". 1940s. Unsigned. $65.00 – 115.00. (Center) Very feminine compact has a silver ball tip which controls the amount of powder sprinklings. Six holes are on the opposite side of the compact. Late 1940s. Signed "Richard Hudnut Paris." $70.00 – 120.00. (Left) The original powder is still in the box. A mirror is on the reverse side of this. 2". Unsigned. 1940s era. $65.00 – 115.00.

Stud-ly steel cut shoe clips with a grosgrain backing. Art Nouveau. Measures 2¾" long by 2¼" wide. Unsigned. $110.00 – 150.00.

Come on baby light my fire! Sporty silver-tone lighter with a tennis player hitting a ball on the green enameled casing. Top and bottom right is signed Manor. Left bottom reads, "By WINDSOR Automatic Higher grade manor lite JAPAN." $45.00 – 85.00.

This statement-making "what not" box is gold tone with a raised flower and leaves. This particular piece is part of a mirrored dresser set from the mid- to late 1960s. Some women used them to store bobby pins or "what nots." Unsigned. $15.00 – 30.00.

A gold rush compact with a floral design done in two tones of golden hues. Oval shaped. Inside mirror missing. 1960s. $50.00 – 70.00.

This 3¼" long by 2¾" wide compact is bedazzling to its beholder. The original powder puff is still inside. Gold "Revlon" name is stamped on a white background. When the compact opens, it reveals a full mirror. Late 1960s to the early 1970s. $95.00 – 115.00.

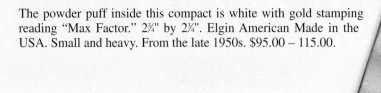

The powder puff inside this compact is white with gold stamping reading "Max Factor." 2¾" by 2¾". Elgin American Made in the USA. Small and heavy. From the late 1950s. $95.00 – 115.00.

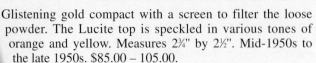

Glistening gold compact with a screen to filter the loose powder. The Lucite top is speckled in various tones of orange and yellow. Measures 2¾" by 2½". Mid-1950s to the late 1950s. $85.00 – 105.00.

A checkerboard of solid and lighter gold squares. Has a full mirror when opened. The original mint green powder puff is stamped "Elgin American." Measures 2¾" by 2¾". Signed "Elgin American Made in the USA." Late 1950s to the mid-1960s. Very heavy. $95.00 – 115.00.

Signed "HARRIET HUBBARD AGER" on the inside bottom right, this compact is simply bedazzling. From the early 1950s to the mid-1960s. Back has a rectangle area for engraving initials. Compact has a full size mirror when opened, and a white, oval powder puff. Stamped in gold on the puff, "Helena Rebinstein." 2¾" by 2¾". $35.00 – 55.00.

Simple gold compact with the original mirror when opened. Has a square powder puff with warm pink tones on both sides. A screen is implemented for loose powder. 2¼" long by 2⅛" wide. Unsigned. Early 1950s to the early 1960s. $55.00 – 85.00.

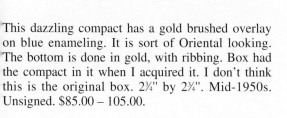

This dazzling compact has a gold brushed overlay on blue enameling. It is sort of Oriental looking. The bottom is done in gold, with ribbing. Box had the compact in it when I acquired it. I don't think this is the original box. 2¾" by 2¾". Mid-1950s. Unsigned. $85.00 – 105.00.

Lightweight compact that has a full, round mirror when opened. A screen for loose powder is inside. When I purchased this, it was in the Fifth Avenue Zell Box. The back of the box reads "Proud Possession of the Particular Woman." Bottom of the compact is done in gold with ribbed circles. Unsigned. $70.00 – 90.00.

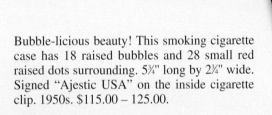

Bubble-licious beauty! This smoking cigarette case has 18 raised bubbles and 28 small red raised dots surrounding. 5¾" long by 2¾" wide. Signed "Ajestic USA" on the inside cigarette clip. 1950s. $115.00 – 125.00.

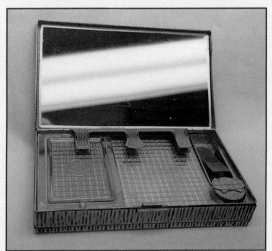

This cigarette case opens to a tri-fold. The gold holder, clip, and lighter are signed "Evans." A place for calling cards, powder, and lipstick are included all on one side. Complete with a full mirror. Very elegant. $120.00 – 150.00.

A calmly curved cigarette case in gold wash over metal. Measures 5¾" by 3¾". Signed "Volupte USA" on each side of the cigarette holder. 1950s. $90.00 – 110.00.

Silver-tone cigarette case with a design that is reminiscent of the Orient. Nice detailing. When opened, there is an elastic holder on each side. 6¼" by 3¼". Unsigned, I'm shocked. 1950s. $100.00 – 140.00.

Highly flammable lighter makes my heart combust! Signed "Ronson" beneath the igniter and inside on the cigarette case's clip holder. 1950s. $75.00 – 105.00.

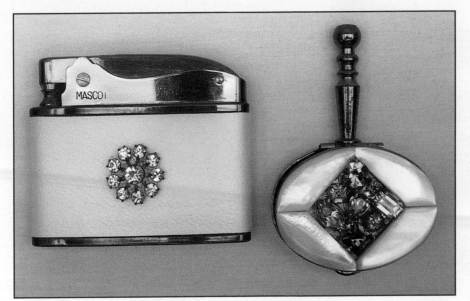

(Left) This lighter is completed in gold toning with white leather and nine small rhinestones that are prong set with one center. Signed "MASCOT" on the top left and bottom left. The bottom right is signed "Super Automatic Light Japan." $45.00 – 85.00. (Right) Four mother-of-pearl chunks overlay the gold top with a variety of colors and shapes of rhinestones. All are prong set by hand. Late 1940s. Unsigned. $50.00 – 90.00.

Look out *Dynasty* era! This belt is 25½" long and 3½" wide. Done in silver, copper, and gold on a silver metallic. Each color has its own 2½" rows of chaton rhinestones. The center stone is 1¾" on the right of the belt. Two rhinestone chains suspend from the bottom of the belt. Late 1970s to the mid-1980s. $80.00 – 120.00.

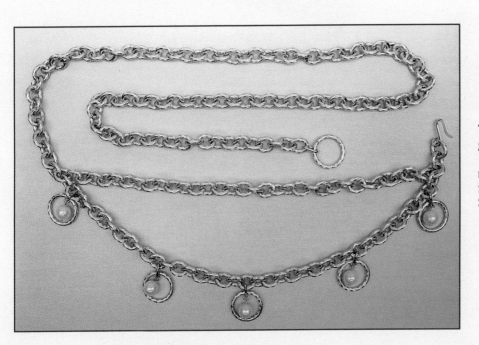

This uptown chain belt made of gold links measures 51" long. A 13" double chain with five gold rings is suspended holding a flexible faux center pearl. 1970s. $40.00 – 70.00.

Dazzling 1¾" show clip from the early 1930s. Unsigned. $35.00 – 65.00.

Plastic hair clip is a bouquet of flowers. Each flower has a glued in aurora borealis center. 1950s. $20.00 – 40.00.

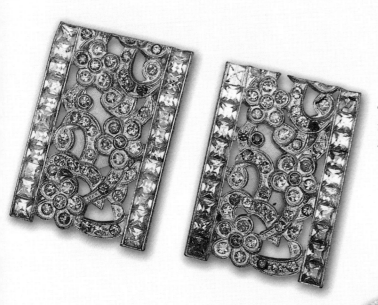

These dress clips are in silver tone and, unfortunately, in poor condition. The baguettes and rhinestones are glued in. 1¾". Early 1930s. $25.00 – 55.00.

Gorgeous dress clips with pavè stones and small, ruby, chaton-cut and baguette-cut stones. 2¼". Early 1930s era. $35.00 – 75.00.

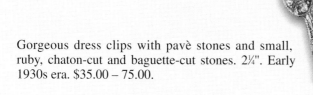

Amazing Aurora Borealis

(Left) Aurora borealis crystals strung on wire for these stunning earrings. One crystal for the center does not have separators. ¾". Unsigned. 1940s to 1950s. $35.00 – 55.00. (Center) Four beads separate the four aurora borealis crystals. One crystal is used for the center. Yellow shades cast nicely. Measures ¾". Unsigned. $35.00 – 65.00. (Right) Signed "LAGUNA." Four beads separate the four aurora borealis crystals. Strung on wire with one crystal center. Back is filigree in silver tone. Absolutely smashing. ¾". 1940s to the 1950s. $40.00 – 70.00.

(Left) Five aurora borealis crystals surround the center crystal. Does not have a bead or crystal to separate. Casts blues. ¾". Unmarked 1940s to 1950s. $40.00 – 70.00. (Center) Five aurora borealis crystals separated by crystal beads. Strung on wire. Casts pinks. Unsigned. 1940s to 1950s. $45.00 – 75.00. (Right) Weighty clip earrings. Two rows of aurora borealis crystals strung on wire with crystal separators, a lone center crystal. Measures ¾". Unsigned. 1940s to 1950s. $45.00 – 85.00.

Pin and clip earrings set. The clip earrings have five aurora borealis crystals, each separated by a small round plastic bead. Strung on wire. Signed "Lisner®" 1940s to 1950s. $45.00 – 80.00.

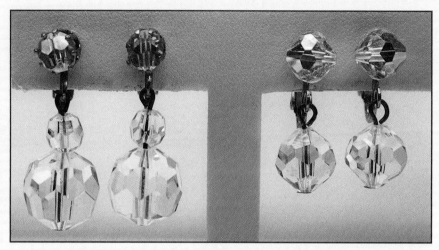

(Left) Two larger aurora borealis crystals dangle from a single, smaller aurora borealis crystal. 1½" long. 1940s to 1950s. $50.00 – 70.00. (Right) Clip earrings measure 1⅛". An aurora borealis crystal drops from the single crystal head. 1940s to 1950s. $35.00 – 65.00.

Pin has aurora borealis crystals strung on wire with crystal bead separators that have silver tips. 1¾". Unsigned. 1940s to 1950s. $95.00 – 135.00.

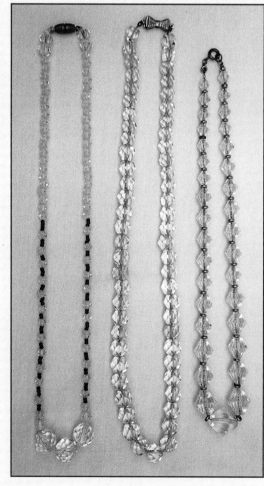

(Left) Clip earrings. Three faux pearls with three aurora borealis crystals with one crystal in the center. Measures 1". Signed "TARA." 1940s to 1950s. $45.00 – 75.00. (Right) Seed pearls, gold beads, and aurora borealis. 1940s to the 1950s. $45.00 – 75.00.

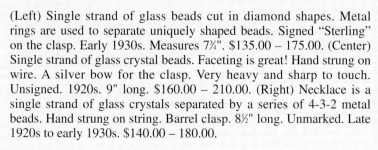

(Left) Single strand of glass beads cut in diamond shapes. Metal rings are used to separate uniquely shaped beads. Signed "Sterling" on the clasp. Early 1930s. Measures 7¾". $135.00 – 175.00. (Center) Single strand of glass crystal beads. Faceting is great! Hand strung on wire. A silver bow for the clasp. Very heavy and sharp to touch. Unsigned. 1920s. 9" long. $160.00 – 210.00. (Right) Necklace is a single strand of glass crystals separated by a series of 4-3-2 metal beads. Hand strung on string. Barrel clasp. 8½" long. Unmarked. Late 1920s to early 1930s. $140.00 – 180.00.

(Outer) Necklace with two strands of sparkling aurora borealis crystals. Each crystal is separated by a gold metal ring that is strung very tightly. Fish-hook clasp with crystals suspended from a silver bar. Measures 5¾". Adjustable chain 3". Unmarked. Late 1940s to 1950s. $140.00 – 180.00. (Center) Clip earrings. Aurora borealis crystals strung on wire. Diamond-shaped beads form a star with a raised, center, round crystal. One of a kind. ¾". Unmarked. 1940s to 1950s. $40.00 – 70.00.

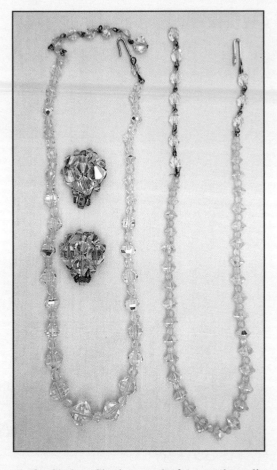

(Left) Choker. Single strand of aurora borealis crystals separated by crystal beads. Very tightly hand strung. 1940s to 1950s. $65.00 – $105.00. (Inner left) Clip earrings. Aurora borealis crystals strung on wire. 1940s to 1950s. $35.00 – 55.00. (Right) Single strand of crystals reflecting the aurora borealis colors. Hand strung on string. Chain is 7". Adjustable chain with fish-hook clasp and seven crystals. 1940s to 1950s. $70.00 – 110.00.

(Left) Single strand of aurora borealis crystals separated by a crystal. Strung extremely tight. 5" long. 1½" adjustable chain. Unsigned. 1940s to 1950s. $85.00 – 120.00. (Right) Beautiful single strand of glass crystals. Each crystal is separated by a glass bead. Cut is greatly detailed and there is a faint hint of aurora borealis. The fish-hook clasp is signed "Laguna." Chain is hand strung on string. Measures 5¾". 1940s to the 1950s era. Heavy. $90.00 –120.00.

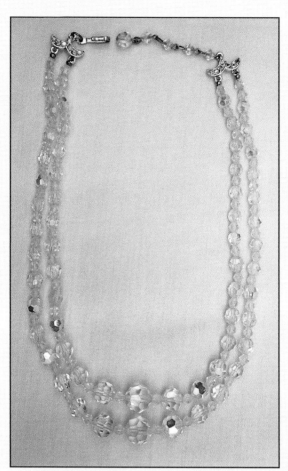

For this necklace, each crystal is separated by a crystal bead. Two strands of stunning, graduated aurora borealis crystals drop from a silver-tone suspension with seven bright rhinestones glued in. Adjustable chain is 2⅛" and the necklace measures 7½". Signed "Lady Ellen" on the fish-hook clasp. 1940s to the 1950s. $130.00 –180.00.

Three rows of brilliant aurora borealis crystals dangle from a silver-tone bar with four glued in rhinestones. One stone is missing on the left side of each silver-tone bar. The crystals are strung very tightly and each is separated by a crystal bead. Measures 6" in length and the fish-hook clasp is 3½". Unsigned, yet uptown chic. 1940s to the 1950s. $150.00 – 200.00.

Three quite lovely strands of aurora borealis crystals are hooked on to a silver bar with an engraved design to finish the bar. Magnificent to wear in the sunshine! Silver-tone, adjustable, fish-hook clasp is 3¼" long, while the necklace measures 6¾". Unsigned. 1940s to the 1950s. $150.00 – 200.00.

Three breathtaking rows of aurora borealis drop from a silver scroll-like top. A rather flexible piece. The fish-hook clasp measures 3¾" in length, while the necklace is 6¼" long. Unsigned. 1940s to the 1950s. $120.00 – 160.00.

Suspended from a silver-tone bar are two strands of aurora borealis crystals in a graduated size. The colors reflect yellows, oranges, and more. Simply elegant. Necklace measures 6¼" and the adjustable, fish-hook clasp is 3¼". Unmarked. 1940s to the 1950s. $120.00 – 150.00.

A silver-tone scroll suspends the splendid, well-cut aurora borealis beads of this necklace. The three strands are sure to reflect the light with an absolute brilliance. 7" long. 1940s to the 1950s. Unmarked. $135.00 – 185.00.

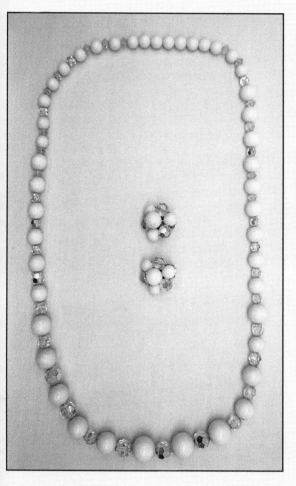

12½" necklace has white plastic beads which are separated by crystal, aurora borealis pieces. Matching clip earrings complete the set. The backing of the earrings is silver tone, with open filigree work. 1940s. Unsigned. $70.00 – 110.00.

(Left) Sparkling clip earrings. Eight crystals surround the large center aurora borealis. Measures ¾". Signed "GERMANY." 1940s. $40.00 – 70.00. (Center) Fine fish-wire strung crystals with a silver backing make up these unmarked, 1", 1940s clips. $40.00 – 70.00. (Right) Clip earrings with silver backings. Nice quality, aurora borealis crystals. The face crystals are tipped with silver pin. ¾". Unmarked. 1940s. $35.00 – 65.00.

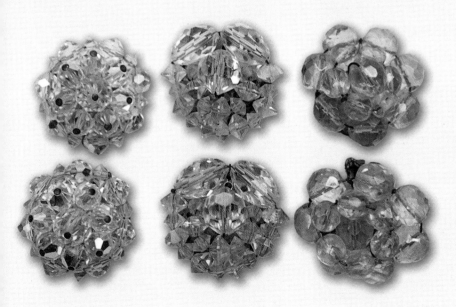

(Left) Silver over metal on the back of these clip earrings. Each face crystal is tipped in silver pins. ¾". Unmarked. 1940s. $40.00 – 70.00. (Center) These, too, are silver over metal clip earrings. Well-worn backing on one earring is down to the metal. 1". Unmarked. 1940s. $40.00 – 70.00. (Right) Clip earrings, all round crystals are strung with black fine wire. 1". Unmarked. 1940s. $35.00 – 65.00.

(Left) Stunning screw-back earrings have a great cast of greens, and nine crystal beads surround the nicely faceted aurora borealis stone. ¾". Signed "STERLING." 1940s. $40.00 – 70.00. (Center) Clip earrings. Silver-tone backing. Dainty aurora borealis encompass a center aurora borealis stone. Unmarked. 1940s. $35.00 – 65.00. (Right) Clip earrings with silver backing. Eight fiery crystals surround the faceted center crystal. These were my Grandma Ault's, but she gave them to me. 1". Signed "GERMANY." 1940s. Priceless.

(Surrounding) Pair of gold-tone clip earrings. Faux pearl and aurora borealis clips with a drop of aurora borealis and pearls finished in gold. 1½" Unmarked. Late 1940s to the early 1950s. $45.00 – 75.00. (Center) Bracelet containing two strands of crystals with a gold button clasp. 3¼" closed. Unsigned. Early 1950s. $105.00 – 135.00.

(Outer) Necklace contains faux pearls and eight crystals strung on a string with a nicely faceted center crystal making nine. The lobster clasp is nicely detailed. 8". Unsigned. Early 1940s. $85.00 – 115.00. (Center) Silver clip earrings. Faux pearls with small aurora borealis in centers of the design. The pearls are tipped with a silver cap. ¾". Unmarked. 1940s. $30.00 – 65.00.

(Left) Necklace with a fish-hook, brass clasp. A single strand of tapered baguette crystals with the aurora borealis casting yellow and purple shades. 7" with 3½" of closure. Unmarked. 1940s. $110.00 – 140.00. (Right) Brass fish-hook clasp attached to aurora borealis rhinestones on each side. Two strands of small crystals with all aurora borealis reminds me of a fresh snowfall. Unmarked. 1940. $105.00 – 135.00.

(Left) A unique and elegant necklace. A large gold-tone fish-hook clasp is attached to a 3" adjustable chain. White glass beads are strung on fine string. 6¼". Unmarked. 1940s. $115.00 – 145.00. (Right) Clip earrings. Silver-tone backing with fancy filigree work. Yellow-green pearls with wonderful, crystal aurora borealis centers. ¾". Unsigned. 1940s. $40.00 – 70.00.

Pennsylvania clip earrings, three strand necklace, and spiral bracelet. The earrings contain silver-tone backing. These pieces show excellent quality of aurora borealis crystal beads. This set is in the original PT, Penn Traffic Co. Distinctive Johnstown, PA, box. This necklace shows great workmanship throughout this 6½" heavy beauty. 1¼" adjustable fish-hook clasp, which is brass and signed "LAGUNA." The other side is a 3" adjustable chain. Five rhinestones begin to suspend 35 aurora borealis crystals. Earrings ¾" and signed "Laguna." Late 1940s. From Penn Traffic Co. Johnstown, PA. $225.00 – 325.00.

(Outer) Unique necklace. 2¼" adjustable gold-tone chain features lemon yellow glass beads. Measures 9¼". Inside the clasp it is signed "PAT PEND." Late 1950s to mid-1960s. $120.00 – 160.00. (Center) Pierced earrings. Three yellow crystal drops. Simple, and are dated back to the 1960s. $30.00 – 50.00.

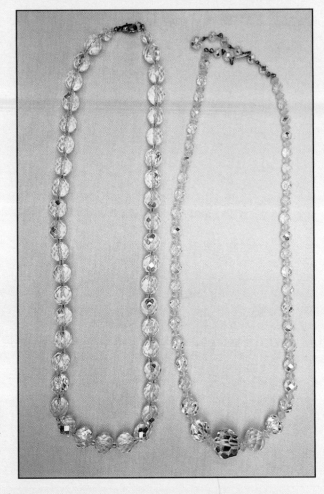

(Left) Nicely faceted glass crystal beads. 1930s to the early 1940s. Hand strung on fish net. $150.00 – 200.00. (Right) A single strand necklace of graduated glass crystal aurora borealis beads with small crystals separating excellent faceted crystals. The center drop is drop-dead gorgeous! Measures 10½" with a 2¾" adjustable chain and fish-hook clasp. Unsigned. 1940s. $120.00 – 150 .00.

(Left) Clip earrings. Radiant colors of small aurora borealis stone suspended from a single hook. 1". Unsigned. Mid- to late 1950s. $35.00 – 45.00. (Right) Clip earrings. Small aurora borealis stone with three chain link drops holding the nice large faceted crystal. 1½". Unmarked. Mid- to late 1950s. $45.00 – 55.00.

(Left) Screw-on earrings. Top has a single, tiny rhinestone glued in. 1½" with three clear crystal beads graduated in size. Signed "JAPAN." Late 1940s to mid-1950s. $25.00 – 40.00. (Right) Clip earrings. Gold-tone backing. Three multicolored crystals with a single lightly colored crystal, held off of a small crystal. 1½" long. Early 1950s. Unsigned. $45.00 – 75.00.

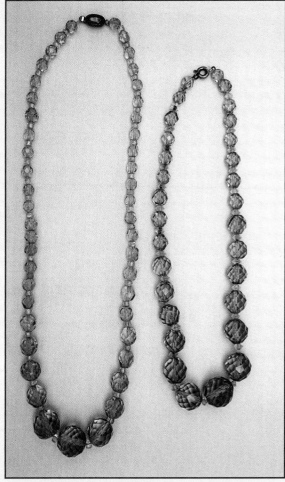

(Left) Beads of four sizes converge to make this splendid, hand-strung necklace. A dark blue glass is used for the clasp. Wonderfully faceted. Mid-1920s to the early 1930s. 9⅛" long. $200.00 – 270.00. (Right) This nicely faceted necklace has three different sizes of graduated beads which are hand strung on string. Each bead is separated by a crystal. Mid-1920s to the early 1930s. Measures 7⅛". $190.00 – 250.00.

Outrageously gorgeous ocean blue crystals are suspended from gold bars. The bars have three rhinestones on each side. One rhinestone is missing. Measures 7". The chain and fish-hook clasp is 3¼". $100.00 – 150.00.

(Outer) This necklace has very lovely shaped crystals. Two rows of aurora borealis crystals droop from beautiful rhodium bars that have four pavè rhinestones in them. A heavy fishhook clasp with a 3" adjustable chain to close. Measures 6". 1940s. Unmarked. $120.00 – 160.00. (Inner) These clip earrings contain crystals which match the aforementioned necklace. They resemble a marquis style. ¾". Unmarked. 1940s. $45.00 – 85.00.

This necklace has two strands of crystals in rainbow colors. Gold beads separate the crystals. The clasp is a simply stunning, bold flower. 10¼" long. 1940s. Unsigned. $200.00 – 280.00.

(Outer) A fun, conversation starter! Strands are suspended from gold bars with multicolored spacers. These pastel prism crystals are in an array of colors. Truly one of a kind. 1940s. Unsigned. 6¾". $170.00 – 230.00. (Inner) The clip earrings match the necklace. ¾". 1940s. Unmarked. $50.00 – 90.00.

(Outer) This necklace has a rhodium back with four pavè rhinestones, two strands of stunning aurora borealis crystals, and a ¾" adjustable chain and fish-hook clasp which is signed "Laguna." Necklace measures 6". 1940s. $120.00 – 170.00. (Inner) Tiny, delicate, aurora borealis crystals are on silver-tone clip earrings. ½". Unsigned. 1940s. $30.00 – 50.00.

(Left) Nicely cut, hand-strung crystals. Each crystal is separated by two beads and one tiny crystal. Measures 8¼". 1920s to the 1930s. Unsigned. $110.00 – 150.00. (Right) A cute choker with finely faceted crystals. Great detailing. Sharp to the touch. Necklace is a single strand of crystals. 1¾" adjustable chain with a large fish-hook clasp. 1930s. Measures 6". $90.00 – 150.00.

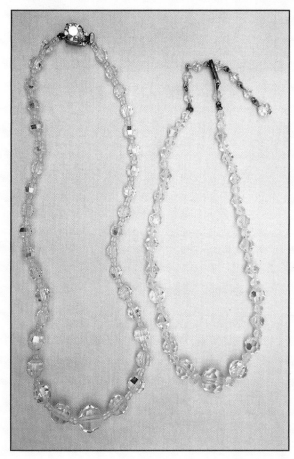

(Left) 1940s beauty. A single strand of aurora borealis crystals with hints of yellow dominating the necklace. A large aurora borealis stone is set in the clasp. Measures 8¼". Unmarked. $120.00 – 160.00. (Right) A tightly strung choker with a single strand of aurora borealis stones. A large center stone is eye catching. 3" adjustable chain, brass fish-hook clasp. Measures 6" long. Unsigned. 1940s. $95.00 – 135.00.

Three strands of aurora borealis crystals are strung on wire. Strands are suspended from a silver bar with five pavè rhinestones. One rhinestone is missing. 3½" adjustable chain, fish-hook clasp. 1940s. Unsigned. $180.00 – 240.00.

Clasp is a prong-set marquis with a single, round rhinestone and two aurora borealis stones. Strung on fishing string. Purples, reds, grays, blues, and greens show through. Each bead has a black spacer. Measures 9½". Unsigned. 1940s. $90.00 – 150.00.

(Left) Beautiful bracelet! This sophisticated bracelet has two strands of aurora borealis crystals. A safety chain is on the clasp. Clasp connects the two small rings of pavè rhinestones. On the right side, two rhinestones are missing. 3½" long. Unsigned. $65.00 – 95.00. (Right) This necklace is fit for a princess. The reflections of the color are brilliant in each crystal. Two strands of aurora borealis drop from a rhodium bar on each side. The bars have four pavè rhinestones each. Measures 6" long with a 2¾" adjustable chain clasp. 1940s. $140.00 – 180.00.

(Left) This uptown chic bracelet has crystals in graduated sizes, separated by crystals. 4¼". Signed "1-2012KCF." 1940s. $90.00 – 140.00. (Right) Choker made with aurora borealis crystals in multiple colors. Sizes are graduated. Strung on wire. Fish-hook clasp is signed "Laguna." Measures 6" with a 3" adjustable chain. 1940s. $110.00 – 140.00.

(Left) Vibrant expansion bracelet with a double strand of aurora borealis crystals. Tightly strung. 1¾". 1940s. $80.00 – 130.00. (Center) These charming clip earrings have one large aurora borealis crystal dropping from a smaller one. Silver clips. Unsigned. Measures ¾". 1940s. $35.00 – 45.00. (Right) This tasteful bracelet is simply elegant. A single strand of aurora borealis crystals strung on wire. Simple crystal drop on each end. 2½" long. Unsigned. 1940s. $45.00 – 65.00.

(Left) These flexible clear beads twist and shake. Signed "Japan." 1940s. 1¼". $40.00 – 60.00. (Right) These clip earrings have aurora borealis crystals which drop like a waterfall. Many crystals are linked by a small chain. Clip is silver tone. 1½". Signed "Laguna." 1940s. $75.00 – 115.00.

The original Laguna box sits behind these pieces. (Left) Heavy, aurora borealis pin with crystals showing aquas, yellows, and pinks. Silver backing. 1940s. 2". Unsigned. $95.00 – 135.00. (Center) This circle pin is so sweet with its nicely sized beads. 1½" in diameter. 1940s. Unsigned. $90.00 – 130.00. (Right) This pin has aurora borealis crystals showing a lot of blues and aquas. Clear beads over silver tips. 1¼" in diameter. ¾" in depth. 1940s. Unsigned. $80.00 – 110.00.

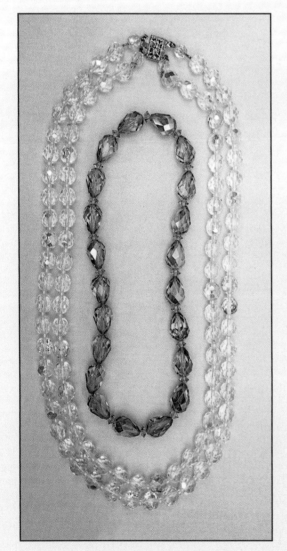

(Outer) Two-strand aurora borealis necklace from the early 1940s. A silver-tone clasp is done in filigree. This flexible necklace is strung on fine silver wire. Weighted. $85.00 – 115.00. (Inner) I would have loved to have seen this necklace before it came apart. Yellow-green crystals are separated by small crystals. Looks like the necklace was broken, and the owner hand tied and knotted it. 1940s. Unsigned. 6." As is: $60.00 – 100.00.

(Left) Silver-tipped, aurora borealis crystals that are heavy and on a silver-tone backing. 1940s. Unsigned. 1½." $85.00 – 115.00. (Right) These clip earrings are hand strung on wire with gold tipping. 1⅛." 1940s. $75.00 – 105.00.

Beads, Beads, Beads

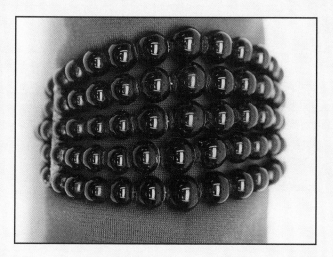

Weighted bracelet. Spiral with five rows of black beads strung on wire. Unmarked. 1960s. $45.00 – 85.00.

(Outer) Jet bead glass. Strung on a very fine linked wire with a large bead on the clasp. 12¼". Mid- to late 1920s. $130.00 – 180.00. (Center) Jet bead glass. Hand strung on black string with a silver clasp with cross design. 7¾". Unsigned. Mid- to late 1920s. $110.00 – 140.00.

This fabulous 22" necklace was probably donned by the flappers of the 1920s. The black jet glass beads are hand strung and knotted. Clear spacers were inserted between each bead. Unsigned. $150.00 – 200.00.

Grand necklace and clip earrings set. Go[l]d-tone scroll bar with two strands of plas[tic] beads in light to dark shades of cranbe[rry] with dark aurora borealis. 7". 3½" adjusta[ble] chain. Earrings measure 1½". Each of t[he] earrings and the fish-hook clasp are sig[ned] "West Germany." Early 1950s. For the s[et] $140.00 – 190.00.

A tasteful, 2001 Christmas gift from my husband. Light pink to deeper shades of grape with plastic beads in three strands. Three marvelous strands drop from a gold-tone bar; each bead has a gold cap. Adjustable chain measures 2¾", necklace is 8", and the earrings are 1¼". The earrings' and the necklace's fish-hook clasps are signed "W. Germany." Early 1950s. No value assigned.

Sophisticated clip earrings and necklace couple. Three strands of yellow and coral plastic beads are suspended from a gold-tone, plastic bar. Each bead is separated by a faux seed pearl. Darling for summertime, fun in the sun! Earrings measure 1". 3" adjustable chain. 8¾" necklace. The earrings and the fish-hook clasp are signed "Japan." 1950s. $85.00 – 125.00.

Remarkable summer necklace and clip earrings duo. Three strands of magnificent coral beads that are separated by small, gold, roped beads. Fish-hook clasp. 6¼" necklace with a 3" adjustable chain. Unsigned. 1950s. $110.00 – 160.00.

Three-tone, purple, plastic beads are strung on heavy string. The strands are dropped from a silver-tone swirl design. 7" long; 1¼" adjustable chain; and the earrings are ¾". Earrings signed "Japan." Late 1950s. $80.00 – 120.00.

Hand-strung, citrine-colored and darker coral beads have gold beads to separate approximately every 3¼". Clasp is six beads with a molded plastic citrine for the center. Earring is 1⅛". Necklace is 12". Necklace clasp and earrings are signed "Made in Western Germany." Early 1950s. $140.00 – 200.00.

Go Steelers! Let's hear it for the Black and Gold! Bold beads! Cute clips! The beads are graduated in size, and each is separated by a golden swirl bead. Earrings, 2¼"; necklace, 8"; adjustable chain, 2¾". Early 1960s. Unsigned. $130.00 – 200.00.

(Outer) Beautiful necklace that is signed "Japan" on the fish-hook clasp. Measures 8"; the adjustable chain is 3¼". Late 1950s. $60.00 – 100.00. (Center) Earrings signed "Miriam Haskell." 1960s. Baroque pearls, bezel-set in gold tone. $100.00 – 150.00.

Katie bought this necklace for me in Saltsburg, Pennsylvania. Great for a summer day in southern Florida. Detailing is typical of Hong Kong. A pattern of two or three beads then separated by a flower. Clasp signed "Hong Kong." Great detail. Early 1950s. 9⅛". No value assigned.

Necklace signed "©Kramer." Single strand of plastic beads are hand strung on string. 8½" long; 3" adjustable chain. 1950s. $100.00 – 140.00.

Necklace strung on rope. Denim blue wooden beads on a 7¼" strand. The tag reads, "Cathy & Marsha for Catherine Stein." Original price of $23.00. 1970s. $50.00 – 90.00.

(Left) Necklace of pear and round-shaped white glass on a hand-knotted string separated by two discs. Necklace measures 6½" with a 3¼" chain and a fish-hook clasp. Signed "MJ WESTERN GERMANY." Late 1940s to early 1950. $105.00 – 135.00. (Right) Hand-strung black glass beads on a black heavy thread. A lot of give between the beads. Looks like Germany though it is unmarked. 6" with a 2¼" adjustable chain. Late 1940s to the early 1950s. $105.00 – 145.00.

Necklace and clip earrings set from the 1970s to the early 1980s. Oh, so *Dallas* and *Dynasty*! Notice one strand is missing. Is this intentional from the previous owner? Strung on string, separated by gold plastic beads. Necklace is 7¾" with adjustable 4⅛" chain. Earrings are 2½" long. Unmarked. $55.00 – 85.00.

Eighteen strands of hand-strung beads measure 7½". The gold-tone floral clasp has a flower's center holding small aqua-colored stones. The leaves hug the strands of beads. Unsigned. 1980s. $140.00 – 180.00.

Silver-tone necklace. 1970s. Measures 8¾" and is unmarked. A fish-hook clasp closes this silver-tone beauty of mint green beads. All are hand strung on a double rope. Hand knotted. $80.00 – 130.00.

Seeing red! Thirty strands of red seed beads. The original tag reads "Pomeroy's $20.00." 1970s. Measures 15". Silver-tone beads and a fish-hook clasp. $120.00 – 190.00.

Two strands of faux pearls, strung on string. Clasp done in gold tone, and a faux pearl in the weighted center. Measures 8". Unsigned. 1970s. Fit for a princess! Elegant, with a hint of bulk. $80.00 – 110.00.

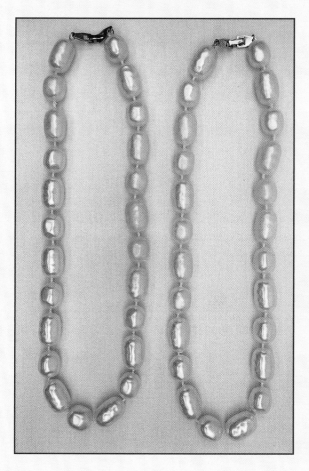

Double trouble! (Left) 8" faux pearl necklaces. Single strand of larger sized pearls strung on a rope. Clasp is gold tone with two chaton cut rhinestones. Unmarked. 1950s. $35.00 – 65.00. (Right) 9" and a silver-tone clasp is the only difference from the left identification. $35.00 – 65.00.

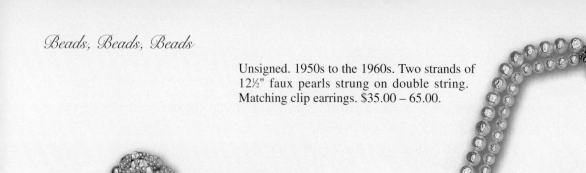

Unsigned. 1950s to the 1960s. Two strands of 12½" faux pearls strung on double string. Matching clip earrings. $35.00 – 65.00.

This three-strand, marvelous, faux white pearl necklace is sure to bring the house down. 9" with a 1¾" clasp signed "JAPAN." Clasp is gold filigree with the back strung on fine wire. Late 1950s to the early 1960s. $85.00 – 135.00.

Single strand of butterscotch plastic beads. Strung on a string of a matching color. Imitates glass. Measures 15½". Late 1940s to mid-1950s. Unsigned. $70.00 – 110.00.

TRIFARI also signed a small "t" on the right side of the adjustable chain, as was used in this particular piece. 8¼" with a 2¾" adjustable chain with a fish-hook clasp. Heavy necklace. Two sizes of faux pearls separated by a small gold-tone ring. Gold-tone barrels embrace the pearls in a pattern of three. Mid-1950s to the early 1960s. $65.00 – 115.00.

Exquisite necklace and matching clip earrings. Four strands of three tones in greens, with golds and aurora borealis. Each bead is separated by a small gold bead. Multiple textures make up the beads. Excellent weight. Measures 8¾" with a 3" adjustable chain. Original paper is red and gold. Tag reads "LaBelle $4.00 plus tax." The clip earrings and fish-hook clasp are signed "Japan." 1950s. $120.00 – 170.00.

Necklace and matching clip earrings. Three strands of multicolored plastic beads are strung on a double string. Each delicate bead is separated by a small, light, topaz colored plastic bead. The necklace measures 7¾" with a 2¾" adjustable chain. Each clip earring is signed "GERMANY." 1940s. $115.00 – 145.00.

"Why don't you build me up, buttercup baby," says a song from the 1960s. This necklace is butter in color. Two strands of plastic beads, aurora borealis, molded plastic, and gold separators. Measures 11¾". Strung tightly, with no give. The clasp is gold tone. So striking! 1950s. $70.00 – 110.00.

People are seeing red for this beauty. Two strands of cranberry plastic beads
are hand strung on cranberry colored string. Unsigned. Measures 9".
1940s to the early 1950s. $55.00 – 85.00.

Light brown, earthy tones make up this three-strand, 8½"
necklace with a 3¼" adjustable chain. The plastic beads are
separated by small aurora borealis beads that are tipped in
gold tone. Signed "JAPAN." Late 1940s to the 1950s.
$60.00 – 90.00.

What a vivid set! Three strands of green beads with aurora bore-
alis and faux pearls separated by small beads. Strung on fish wire.
Measures 6¼" with a 2¾" adjustable chain. Clip earrings to match.
All pieces are weighted. Unmarked. Mid-1940s to the 1950s.
$75.00 – 115.00.

Flower Power

This is a collection of Japanese thorn roses from the 1960s. (Left to Right) 1. Black enameling for the flower with green enameling for the leaves and stem. Measures 2¼". Unsigned. 2. A yellow rose with green enameling for the leaves and gold stem. Yellow signifies loyalty. 2¾". Unsigned. 3. Gold-tone plated, red enameled rose with light green/brown leaves and a gold stem. 2¾". 4. I've never seen a green rose before. Grass green enameling over gold tone for the flower and leaves, with a gold stem. 2¾". All prices range between: $20.00 – 45.00.

Luxurious, gold accented, thorn roses. (Left) Measures 2¾". Signed "Giovanni" on the stem. 1960s. $25.00 – 45.00. (Center) Off-white, plastic flower with a gold-tone leaf on the stem. 2½". Unsigned. 1960s. $12.00 – 17.00. (Right) A dark red, glossy rose with gold-tone leaves. 2¾". Unsigned. 1960s. $18.00 – 25.00.

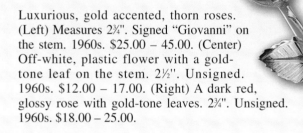

Some may call this a collection of funeral flowers because of the first black flower. (Left) Black molded plastic rose with a gold stem and leaves. Great depth and detail. 2½". 1960s. $20.00 – 40.00. (Center) Pretty, purple rose. Rather heavy. Light purple, almost periwinkle. The entire pin is done in enameling. 1¾" diameter. 1960s. $18.00 – 22.00. (Right) Five dark green emerald leaves with a center of light aqua. Dark green enameling is used for the leaves. 2⅛". 1960s. Unsigned. $17.00 – 23.00.

Spring fury! (Left) A four petal flower with a green stamen and leaves. 1½". 1960s. $15.00 – 20.00. (Right) Heavy hitter! Three dainty flowers, enameled in pink, with green and yellow stamen. Three emerald green leaves and one stem. 1960s. Short of 3". Unsigned. $25.00 – 45.00.

Perfect, pink accented posies. (Left) A pink rhinestone is utilized for the center of this three dimensional flower. Gold trimming complements the pink and green casts well. Reminds me of sugary icing! Short of 3". 1960s. Unsigned. $18.00 – 22.00. (Center) This baby bouquet is simply stunning. 1940s. Signed "Austria." 2¼". $20.00 – 25.00. (Right) Pink plastic flowers with yellow center. One green enamel leaf on the gold-tone stem. 3⅛". 1960s. Unsigned. $15.00 – 20.00.

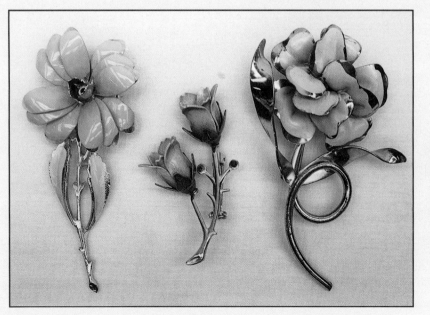

A collection of pastel colored roses. (Left) Four groups of light purple petals with a gold-tone center. Two green enameled leaves complement the stem. 1960s. 3⅜". Unsigned. $22.00 – 32.00. (Center) Light purple and green enameling comprise this flower. 1960s. 2¼". Unsigned. $15.00 – 18.00. (Right) Heavy! This light pink enameled rose has raised leaves with gold-tone trim. 1960s. 3¼". Unsigned. $22.00 – 32.00.

A collection of Kimoto Japanese/Mid-American posies. Kudos to the treeologist, Rob Barkley, for this catchy name. (Top Left) Green enameling over gold tone for a five petal, single flower. 2". 1960s. $20.00 – 25.00. (Bottom Left) Jagged edges, so sharp to touch! Simple pea green enameled flower with five pink leaves surrounding the center. 1⅛" diameter. 1960s. Unsigned. $15.00 – 19.00. (Center) This flower has a multitude of greens used to exemplify its beauty. 2". 1960s. $20.00 – 25.00. (Right) Radiant yellow flower that is cutting to the touch. Ten petals in all, made of sharp metal. Enameled yellow with a center of two golden twigs. Two topaz-colored rhinestones distinguish the piece. 1960s. 3¼". Unsigned. $20.00 – 25.00.

Absolute ocean blue vibrancies. (Left) Faux pearl is set for the center. 2¾". Early 1960s. Silver-tone stem. $20.00 – 40.00. (Right) The gold-tone stem is enameled in a deep yellow. Two faux pearls are set in the center of the flower. 3⅛". Early 1960s. Unsigned. $20.00 – 40.00.

Four good 'ole garden-variety daisies. All unmarked, from the 1960s, gold tone over metal. All measure 1¾". All: $20.00 – 35.00.

Glossy, white silver medallions. (Left) 1960s. 2½". Signed "Sarah Cov." $22.00 – 40.00. (Center) 1¾". Unsigned. 1960s. $12.00 – 20.00. (Right) 2½". 1960s. Unsigned. $12.00 – 22.00.

(Left) Four-petal flower with black and white enameling. 2". 1960s. Unsigned. $20.00 – 35.00. (Right) 2½". Gold-tone beads for the stamen. 1960s. Unsigned. $18.00 – 25.00.

Crazy blue brilliance! Five petals of ocean blue enameling over gold tone with a gold center and gold stem holding two leaves. 3¾". Signed "Sarah Coventry." 1960s. $35.00 – 55.00.

Memorial Day madness/Fourth of July fiestas! (Left) 2¼". 1960s. Unsigned Red, white, and blue enameling over gold tone. Cute. $20.00 – 40.00. (Right Red, white, and blue enameling over gold tone with great lattice work. 2¾" diameter. 1960s. Unsigned. $20.00 – 40.00.

(Left) Americana flower. 1960s. Diameter is 3½". $20.00 – 30.00. (Right) Daisy. 2½" in diameter. $20.00 – 30.00.

America, United. (Left) Flower pin/brooch. Red, white, and blue enameling over gold toning. Done in 3-D with a center of white. 1960s. 2¾". $20.00 – 40.00. (Right) Red, white, and blue enameling over gold tone with a flat blue 1¼" center. 2½". Unsigned. 1960s. $20.00 – 30.00.

Green greatness! (Left) 3". Shades of grass green enameling over gold tone. Nice depth. 1960s. $20.00 – 40.00. (Right) Flower pin. I've never seen such a nice green sunflower. Detailing focused in the petals and center. 2½". 1960s. $20.00 – 40.00.

Obviously orange and ridiculously red! (Left) Six enameled orange petals with a small yellow center. 3". 1960s. $20.00 – 35.00. (Right) Six red enameled petals in a set of two with a white center. Leaves look heart shaped. 2". 1960s. $15.00 – 20.00.

(Left) Winter white poinsettia brooch. White enameled petals in pairs of two. Seedy center, crude detailing. 3¼". 1960s. Unsigned. $20.00 – 30.00. (Right) Poinsettias are my favorite. Eight red enameled petals in an overlapping pattern with a raised center in yellow. A small green leaf and stem. 1960s. 3". Unsigned. $20.00 – 40.00.

Basically black and wonderfully white combo. 1" depth. 3½". 1960s. Unsigned. Enameling. $25.00 – 45.00.

(Left) Large flower pin in white. Overlapping petals done in enameling. Five brown stones for the center. Weighted. 2½". Unsigned. 1960s. $20.00 – 30.00. (Right) Mother-of-pearl sheen for the petals with six ocean blue, prong-set rhinestones for the center. Unique center. The Virgin Mary can be seen in the center. 1½". 1950s. $20.00 – 45.00.

Red, white, and blue Americana daisy pin that has golden-toned plating. It measures 3" long by ¾" wide. 1960s. Unsigned. $15.00 – 35.00.

Oblique sunflower stretch pin is 4" long and 2½" wide. Unsigned. $10.00 – 20.00.

Not a brown-eyed Susan, but rather, a brown leafed, white-eyed daisy. 3½" long and 2" wide. 1960s. Unsigned. $10.00 – 20.00.

Three spectacular sunflowers. All from the 1960s; all unsigned. (Left) Pea green enameled leaves with an ocean blue center. 2¾" by 1½". $10.00 – 20.00. (Center) Twelve white lacquered petals on this pretty daisy. $5.00 – 10.00. (Right) 2¾" by 2¾". $12.00 – 22.00.

Ocean mist, 3-D flower pin with enameling. 2½" wide by 3¾" long. 1960s. Unsigned. $12.00 – 22.00.

4¾" long by 2½" wide. 1960s. Unsigned. Very pretty. $12.00 – 22.00.

Vivacious buttercup pin in varied pink hues. Heavy. 4" long by 2½" wide. Signed "WEISS©." 1960s. $30.00 – 60.00.

Delectable daisy with a gold-tone plate. 1½" by 2¾". 1960s. Unsigned. $10.00 – 20.00.

A raised, yellow enamel center for this big, beautiful creature. 3¾" long by 1¾" wide. $12.00 – 22.00.

A fine specimen indeed. Eight rhinestones surround the magnificent large center stone. 2½" long by 2" wide. $18.00 – 28.00.

Marvelous, large-leafed flower pin. 2¾" long by 2" wide. 1960s. Signed "Eb." $20.00 – 40.00.

Weighty! Salmon-colored petals with a yellow center. 3½" by 2¼". 1960s. Unsigned. $12.00 – 22.00.

Lovely flower pin with three small aurora borealis centers. One of the centers is missing. 4½" long by 2" wide. Unsigned. $20.00 – 30.00.

I'm surprised this pin is unsigned. 1960s. 2½" wide by 4" long. Five large petals rim inner leaves in small, precise shapes. $18.00 – 28.00.

Heavy salmon-colored petals with a yellow center. 3¾" long by 2¼" wide. 1960s. $15.00 – 25.00.

Plain Jane daisy. 2¾" by 1½" wide. 1960s. $8.00 – 18.00.

Delightful daisy brooch with a metal base and enameling. 4¼" by 2½". Unsigned. 1960s. $12.00 – 22.00.

Yay for yellow! This striking flower measures 3¾" long by 2½" wide. 1960s. Unsigned. $20.00 – 30.00.

Spotted dahlia with seven white petals drizzled with black. 1960s. Unsigned. 2½" wide by 3¾" long. $17.00 – 27.00.

A black rose is a rose like none other. Heavy. Measures 3" long by 1½" wide. 1960s. $15.00 – 30.00.

Couple cuties. 3½" long by 2" wide. 1960s. $18.00 – 28.00.

Pea green petals make this a pretty posy (kudos to Rob Barkley, treeologist extraordinaire, for the awesome alliteration). 1960s. Unsigned. 2½" by 3¾". $12.00 – 22.00.

Darling daisy. 3¾" long by 2" wide. 1960s. $12.00 – 22.00

(Left) Pretty in pink with a white center. 2" by 2". Unsigned. 1960s. $8.00 – 18. (Right) What a saucy Brown-eyed Susan in pink! 1960s. 2". 12.00 – 20.00.

(Left) 3½" in diameter. Ready for red in this poinsettia type flower pin. 1960s. $15.00 – 30.00. (Right) What an explosive riveting red and brown daisy with enameled green center! 1960s. $15.00 – 25.00.

Flower pin, 1960s. Coral colors with a gold-tone stem. A green enameled leaf twists to the left side. 3-D effect. $15.00 – 25.00.

Daisy flower pins from the 1960s. Each has eight yellow petals with orange centers. Each measures 2½". $15.00 – 25.00.

Orchids abound! This shows that there are many creative designs for these lovely flowers. 1960s. $12.00 – 25.00.

(Left) Two-tone blue green petals with jagged ends. Detailed center. 1960s. $12.00 – 20.00. (Center) What a pretty, baby blue daisy with a deep blue center! 1960s. $12.00 – 20.00. (Right) Two-tone blue green petals with jagged ends. Solid dark blue center. 1960s. $12.00 – 20.00.

(Left) White enameling over six metal petals in three dimensions. Center is a faux pearl. Early 1960s. $40.00 – 70.00. (Right) This gold and white flower pin has sharp contrasts of gold and white. Early 1960s. $40.00 – 70.00.

(Left) This 1960s flower pin has taupe enameling over gold with three green leaves. The center is made of aurora borealis with gold beads. $40.00 – 70.00. (Right) This 1960s flower pin is made of mother-of-pearl and simply shimmers. Great coloring. $40.00 – 70.00.

Both of these lovely flower pins are from the 1960s. (Left) Great detail on this green enameled pin. $30.00 – 60.00. (Right) A pretty, contrasting flower. $30.00 – 60.00.

(Top) Gold-tone flower pin from the 1960s. $30.00 – 70.00. (Right) The original Coro tag is still attached to this lovely flower. Simply delectable. $40.00 – 80.00.

(Left) This flower pin is a retro 1960s find. Gold tone. Very popular in department stores at that time. $40.00 – 70.00. (Right) This flower pin is done in gold tone with small three-dimensional leaves. $40.00 – 70.00.

These flower pins are a retro, 1960s find. Silver tone. Very popular in department stores at that time. $40.00 – 70.00.

This 1960s flower brooch has five silver tone petals with a center aurora borealis stone. $50.00 – 90.00.

Glimmer in Gold Tone

A swinging, retro 1970s discovery! This striking necklace was a gift from my mother-in-law. Ornately carved drops dangle from a remarkable pendant. Pendant is gold plating over metal. What a weighty piece! 12½" long; center 2¾" wide. Signed on the center and center of drop, "©Donall StannART." $200.00 – 250.00.

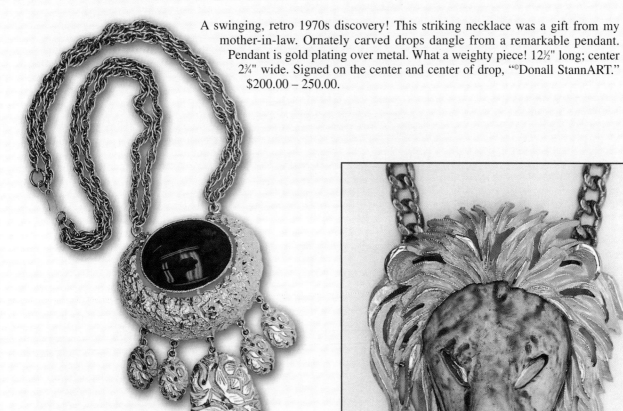

A ferocious find from the 1970s would make the perfect gift for any cat lover. This wild, large life-like lion pendant is suspended from a dazzling linked 9¾" chain. This little kitty is gold plated with a bone colored, molded plastic face. Signed "©RAZZA." $250.00 – 300.00.

What a splashy sunburst from the bold 1970s! This is my mother's absolute favorite summer sun. This Mr. Sun is blindingly big; the actual sunburst measures an astounding 5" in width and is upheld by a 15¾" chain. It's a weighty wear. Signed "KENNETH© Lane." $500.00 – 800.00.

Cleopatra, coming at you! This exotic psuedo-Egyptian necklace is equipped with nine squares accompanied by teardrops. In the center of the squares and drops are circular faux turquoise stones. Amazingly, this 1970s cultural catch is unsigned. The chain is 8" long and both the chain and appendages are gold plated. $120.00 – 160.00.

1970s era. She sells seashells by the seashore! Oh yes, this sandy find may be unsigned, but it resembles early Kenneth Lane. The 5" gold-plated chain is complete with five saucy seashells which are also gold plated. $110.00 – 150.00.

This gold plated goodie could spice up many an outfit. The graduated Omega style chain possesses a blood red cabochon center with matching clip earrings. These classy clips are 1½" in length. Signed "Monet" on the clips of the earrings and clasp of the necklace. 1970s. $110.00 – 150.00.

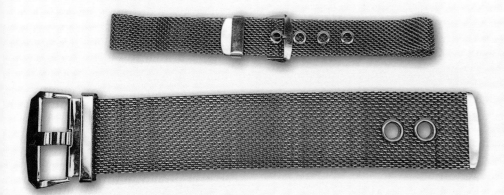

(Top) A charismatic choker screams 1970s. Measures 14¾" when opened. Unsigned. Gold plated. $40.00 – 80.00. (Bottom) Another hot, 1970s pleasure that is 1½" wide. Two holed, adjustable, gold plated, chain bracelet. Unsigned. $30.00 – 60.00.

Fun for all! Lucky number 13. Thirteen bold, bouncy, beads hang in a pattern of faux pearl, gold, and gunpowder from the bulky 18½" chain. Fish-hook clasp, so typical of the 1970s. Unsigned. $40.00 – 70.00.

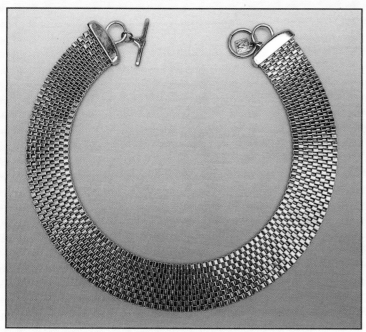

This head-turning necklace has a clasp composed of rhinestones on a bulky, costume, herringbone chain. The emerald green cabochon drop has an open back. Unsigned. $60.00 – 120.00.

This 1970s necklace makes many women want to play that funky music because it flatters any neckline. Gold plated. Very heavy and measures 1" in width. The gold tag is stamped with Ann Klein's logo and signature. $75.00 – 115.00.

Merry molded clear plastic, smoked with faux pearls and a gold-tone cap enclosure. Measures 3½". 1970s. Unsigned. $60.00 – 120.00.

Haute stuff, baby tonight! This pin is certainly a class act with its double trouble mesh rings held together by small, solid gold plates. 2¼" of power pin! 1970s. Signed "Napier." $45.00 – 85.00.

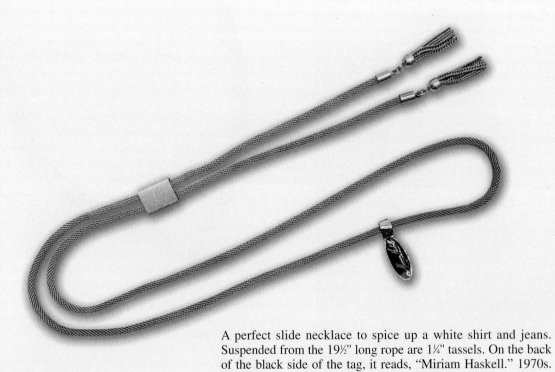

A perfect slide necklace to spice up a white shirt and jeans. Suspended from the 19½" long rope are 1¼" tassels. On the back of the black side of the tag, it reads, "Miriam Haskell." 1970s. Signed "Miriam Haskell." $110.00 – 160.00.

Teddy bear, teddy bear, turn around; teddy bear, teddy bear, touch the ground! Wow! This stunning teddy bear pin is gold plated with exquisitely detailed eyes, paws, nose, and ears. 3½" long and 2½" wide. Oh, that bow just finishes this cutie! Heavy and unmarked. Rhinestones are glued. 1970s. $70.00 – 100.00.

These magical clip-on earrings really hit the spot. Glued in rhinestones in black and crystal colors. 2¾" long and 1¼" wide. Unsigned. 1970s. $50.00 – 80.00.

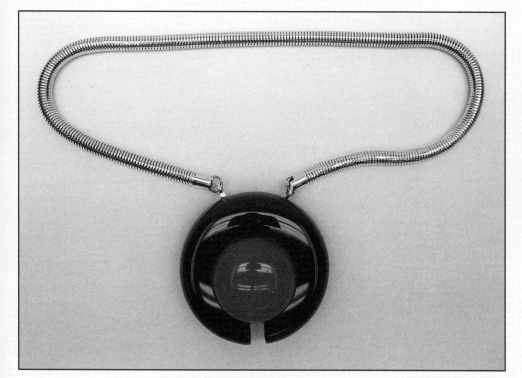

Lovely Lanvin France gold-plated rope chain necklace measures 8¾" and has a red on black centered drop. The cut out drop is 2¾". Late 1960s to the early 1970s. $120.00 – 180.00.

The black lacquered center of this gold-plated necklace is offset by its 10½" chain. Fishhook clasp. Early 1970s. Signed "©Monet" on the back of the center. $70.00 – 110.00.

Charming choker/necklace is gold plated with seven clear rhinestones glued shallow cups. Measures 17¼" long. Unsigned. Early 1970s. $45.00 – 85.00.

A pin with punch! It is gold plated with 17 one-inch chains swinging from the detailed, half diamond shaped pin. Gold beads add nice detailing. 4¾" from top to bottom. Unsigned. Late 1960s to early 1970s. $60.00 – 110.00.

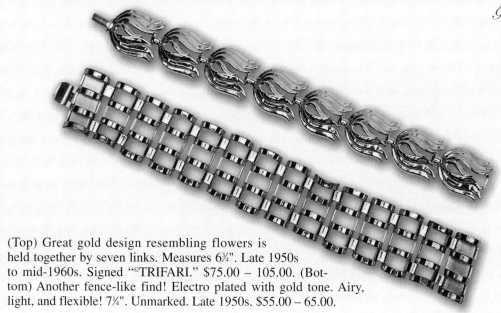

(Top) Great gold design resembling flowers is held together by seven links. Measures 6¾". Late 1950s to mid-1960s. Signed "©TRIFARI." $75.00 – 105.00. (Bottom) Another fence-like find! Electro plated with gold tone. Airy, light, and flexible! 7¼". Unmarked. Late 1950s. $55.00 – 65.00.

Expand your horizons with this nice quality, 1¼" wide gold-tone mid-1960s to the mid-1970s unsigned expansion bracelet. $60.00 – 90.00.

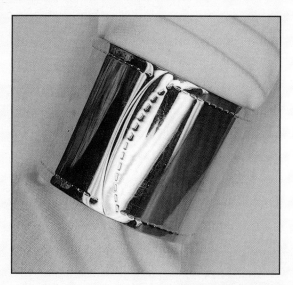

Creative cuff with deep engraving and a simple design. Gold-tone plating. 1¾" wide. Signed "Monet©" in center inside. Mid-1960s to the mid-1970s. $110.00 – 150.00.

Great detail. Should have been signed. Cuff with hinge. A rose on each side without the thorns. Mid-1960s to mid-1970s. $85.00 – 105.00.

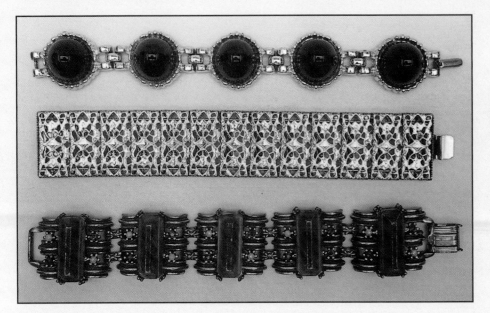

(Top) Five, black plastic cabochons are set in gold tone circles. Cabochons are ¾" high and the bracelet measures 7" long. Unsigned. 1950s. $110.00 – 140.00. (Center) Signed "©Sarah Cov." 1950s. Links are mobile. $90.00 – 130.00 (Bottom) Antique gold tones with five links holding a small emerald and faux pearl with an amber Lucite center. 7⅛". 1950s. Unsigned. $130.00 – 170.00.

Clip earrings with matching bracelet. Plating is gold-tone wash over metal. Antique gold plated look. Four links of domed Lucite hold faux seed pearls with gold sparkles. Resembles water. Bulky and heavy. Bracelet: 7½" long by 2" wide. Earrings: 1¼". 1950s. Unsigned. $140.00 – 200.00.

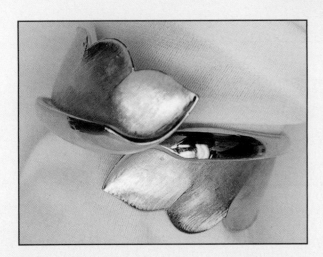

Gold-tone electroplating. Weighty. Nice hinge cuff bracelet. Stamped "TRIFARI©" on hinge. Mid-1960s to mid-1970s. $100.00 – 130.00.

Thirteen small baguettes are in the middle of the bracelet's four links. Very beautiful, very crowd pleasing. 6¼" long. Mid-1960s to early 1970s. Signed "TRIFARI PAT PEND" on the clasp. $90.00 – 120.00.

Chunky, clunky, funky! Fabo 1950s find. (Top) Silver-tone chain bracelet with seven molded plastic dangles. Two have filigree holders. 7" long. Two charms are missing and should have had filigree. Unsigned. $80.00 – 120.00. (Center) Gold-tone chain with five worldly charms that have faux pearls set in each. 7¼" long. 1950s. Unsigned. $80.00 – 110.00. (Bottom) Six molded plastic charms with three gold-tone twisted leaf charms. 7⅛". Signed "Coro." 1950s. $115.00 – 135.00.

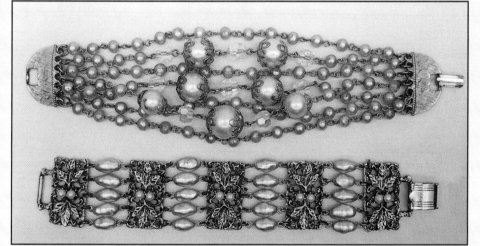

(Top) Seven strands of faux pearls in small and large sizes. Three plastic, and three aurora borealis on three chains are used to separate the sizes. 1950s. Unsigned. $110.00 – 150.00. (Bottom) Five antique gold links with two small, faux seed pearls glued in links to five faux fresh water pearls. 6¾". 1950s. Signed "Celebrity New York." $125.00 – 165.00.

(Top) Gold chains hold a single perfume dauber. A faux jade center is held by a frightful dragon. 5½" long. Early 1960s. $110.00 – 150.00. (Bottom) Beautiful 7¾" bracelet. Early to mid-1960s. Unsigned. $80.00 – 100.00.

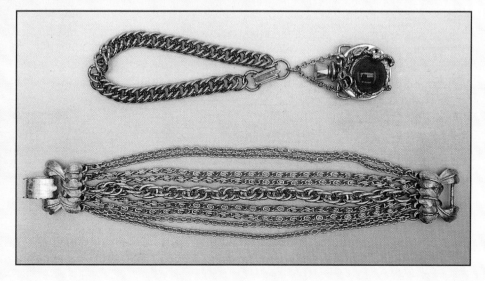

(Left) Two-tone gold with leaves. Complete with a gold-tone vine. Measures 2¼". Early to mid-1970s. Unmarked. $40.00 – 70.00.
(Right) This pretty plant has six leaves brushed in gold with a vein design on each. 2¾." Early to mid-1970s. Unsigned. $35.00 – 65.00.

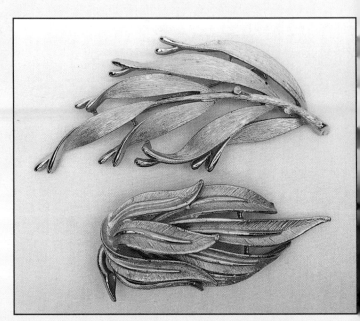

(Top) Lisner brooch is gold-tone wash over metal with a feathered vine of brushed leaves. 1970s. 3¼". $50.00 – 80.00. (Bottom) Mid-1960s to the early 1970s Coro brooch. 2½". $50.00 – 80.00.

(Top and Bottom) Seeing double! These Avon bows have a ribbon of rhinestones in the center. Circa 1980. 2¼". $35.00 – 55.00.

(Top) Gold electroplated bow pin. 2¾". Solid, with cut out hoops. Mid-1960s to the late 1960s. $55.00 – 85.00. (Bottom) Bow pin from the mid- to late 1960s. Unmarked. Gold tone. 2⅛". $40.00 – 60.00.

(Top) Gold wash over metal. Open circle with a ribbon. Five faux pearls are glued. 2¼". Mid- to late 1960s. Signed "Lisner." $55.00 – 75.00. (Bottom) 2" pin that is unmarked is from the 1960s. A sort of four leaf clover. $50.00 – 70.00.

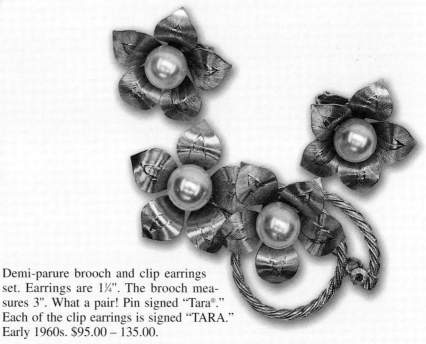

Demi-parure brooch and clip earrings set. Earrings are 1¼". The brooch measures 3". What a pair! Pin signed "Tara®." Each of the clip earrings is signed "TARA." Early 1960s. $95.00 – 135.00.

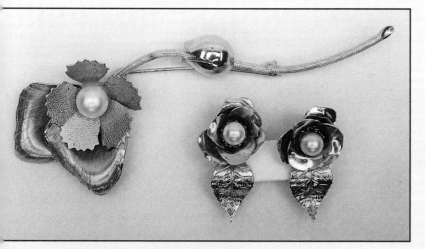

Top) Perfect, long-stemmed flower pin that is holding a glued-in faux pearl. What a long stem! 5." Early 1960s. $30.00 – 50.00. (Bottom) Pretty rose clip earrings with a center pearl, and leaves with an etched vein design. 1¼". Unsigned. Early 1960s. $25.00 – 40.00.

An antique gold brooch with dogteeth. Four aurora borealis stones with a fancy, closed filigree design on the back. A nicely done, hand-painted center of two flowers in black and gold. 2¼". Mid- to late 1950s. Unsigned. $65.00 – 95.00.

Eight small seed pearls are set in the antique gold border. A blue, marbleized center of plastic. Open backed. 2¼". Unmarked. Mid-1950s to the early 1960s. $65.00 – 95.00.

(Top) Heavy, gold-tone brooch with a rope design. Two solid rings are in the center. 3⅜". Late 1960s to the mid-1970s. Unmarked, unbelievable. $65.00 – 95.00. (Bottom) 2¼", unsigned pin. Open latticework is used on the ribbon design. Early 1960s to the mid-1970s. $45.00 – 65.00.

A one-sided, knotted ribbon with a nice brushed design. 2½". Mid-1960s to the early 1970s. Signed "Coro." $65.00 – 85.00.

Very heavy, very gold wash over sterling. Stamped "NAPER STERLING." 1¾". Early 1960s. $80.00 – 130.00.

Demi-parure pin and clip earrings set with petals on each bend of the sternum of the flower. 1½" pin, earrings are ½". Each of the clip earrings and the flower are stamped "Trifari©." 1960s. $80.00 – 130.00.

Unique looking brooch with an open twig design with a border and center of raised, gold beads. 2¼". 1960s. Signed "©LISNER." $65.00 – 85.00.

A cool, lightening design with a center of pavè rhinestones. 1¾". Unmarked. 1960s. $60.00 – 80.00.

Peacefully pretty brooch with pearls glued in shallow basins. Double stemmed. 2¼". Signed "TRIFARI©." 1960s. $60.00 – 80.00.

Looks like fall! Gold wash over metal. Two leaves with a center vein and stems holding glued rhinestones. 2½". 1960s. Unsigned. $55.00 – 75.00.

Three glued-in aurora borealis stones with two black glass hearts in a pear-shaped cut hug the center vine design. 2¼". Late 1960s. $60.00 – 90.00.

(Top) The heaviest x-ed bar pin. 3½". Unsigned. 1970s. $50.00 – 80.00. (Bottom) 2¾" bar pin in antique gold wash over metal. 1970s. Unsigned. Weighty. $50.00 – 80.00.

(Left) Dynamic wreath pin with a top made of glued-in rhinestones. Late 1940s. Unsigned. 1¾". $115.00 – 135.00. (Right) Gold plated brooch. Four set stones. A cute clef and note over a bass. 3¼" long. Unsigned. 1940s. $150.00 – 180.00.

Left) Clip earrings from the late 1940s to the early 1950s. 1⅛". Three faux pearls with four aurora borealis stones in this leafy design. $30.00 – 40.00. (Right) 1940s – 1950s. Five petals with gold tips and silver centers. Each petal is topped with an aurora borealis stone. A center of stones and a faux pearl. $65.00 – 5.00.

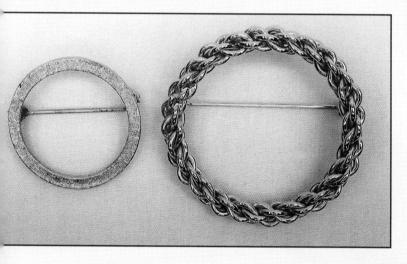

(Left) This circle pin is unmarked and from the early to mid-1960s. 1⅛". $25.00 – 35.00. (Right) This circle pin is unsigned. 1½" rope design from early to mid-1960s. $40.00 – 60.00.

(Top) A single heart dangles from the floral bar. Locket opens. Mid- to late 1950s. 2⅛". Signed "©Lillian Vernon." $60.00 – 90.00. (Bottom) The bar pin is unmarked with a knot on a twig. Gold toning. 1960. 2". $30.00 – 40.00.

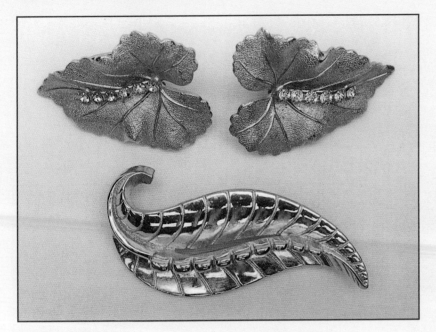

(Top) Six prong-set rhinestones are in the center of this leaf. 1½". Early 1960s. Unsigned. $30.00 – 50.00. (Bottom) Pin is 2⅛". Signed "©Sarah Cov." Late 1960s. Leaf with a raised vein center. $45.00 – 75.00.

Art pin. The back is gold tone. Etched designs. 1¾". Stamped "Spain." Early to mid-1950s. $90.00 – 130.00.

(Left) Pink enameling with a raised round design of a deep pink rose. 2⅛". Unsigned. Early to late 1950s. $25.00 – 45.00. (Right) Cute Coro pin. 1½". Mid-1950s to early 1960s. Gold-tone border with four small rhinestones at the edge of the cut outs. $40.00 – 70.00.

(Left) 1¼." Mid- to early 1970s. Signed, though too hard to read. $25.00 –55.00. (Right) Clip earrings on the original Monet holder. Clip stamped "Monet." Early to mid-1970s. 1⅜". $25.00 – 55.00.

(Top) Clip earrings with three open filigree panels. Topped off with a gold-tone clip. 1⅜". Signed "©Sarah Cov. Pat. Pend." Late 1960s to the early 1970s. $25.00 – 55.00. (Bottom) Coro clip earrings. 1⅛". $25.00 – 55.00.

Left) Gold tone bracelet. Does not open. 1970s. nsigned. $20.00 – 40.00. (Center) Bracelet cuff ith bezel setting. 1⅛". Green faux stone for the cen- r. 1970s. Unsigned. $40.00 – 70.00. (Right) inged and safety-chained bracelet. Lightweight. ate 1960s. Signed "Coro." $40.00 – 80.00.

Heavy chain links with mother-of-pearl, wood, polished stone, and gold-tone charms. 7". Mid-1960s to the early 1970s. Gift from my mother-in-law. No value assigned.

(Left) Bracelet is gold-toned with hinges. Design of engraved diamonds. Signed "KENNETH LANE." 1960s to the early 1970s. $105.00 – 135.00. (Center) CORO PAT PEND bracelet. Looks like Miami to me! Seashells, coral, and faux seed pearls. 1960s. $100.00 – 130.00. (Right) Hinged, gold-tone bracelet from the late 1960s. The design is a heavy knot in a twist. $100.00 – 130.00.

Clip earrings and necklace done in gold tone. All oval rhinestones. This set is true royalty. Necklace center is 3¾" with a 5¼" chain and 2½" adjustable chain with a ball on the end. Earrings measure 1" with one being signed "TRIFARI." $130.00 – 180.00.

(Outer) Unsigned necklace measuring at the center 3½" with a 5¾" chain. Late 1940s to the 1950s. Four weighted gold leaves detailed with two copper petaled flowers with silver tipped leaves. All dangle from the vine. $105.00 – 125.00. (Center) Bow pin signed "Monet Sterling." Measures 2¼". 1940s. Done in copper and gold tones. $80.00 – 120.00.

(Top) CORO necklace. 1950s. Center is 3¼" with a 5¾" chain. Done in gold tone. Center holds two small links of baguettes with a larger center. $95.00 – 135.00. (Center) TRIFARI PAT PEND gold-tone necklace. Center 4" with seven links of diamond shaped rhinestones between the two gold-tone loops. Chain is 4¾". Early 1950s. $95.00 – 135.00. (Bottom) "PAT TRIFARI PEND" is on the back of the 2¾"center with pavè baguettes of three rings. The adjustable chain measures 2½" with a ball on the end, a fish-hook clasp to close. Early 1950s. $95.00 – 135.00.

(Top) 2¼" bird pin. This heavy golden beauty offers red and crystal rhinestones on the head with an emerald colored eye. Wing and tail enameled in dark blue. Mid-1960s to the early 1970s. Unsigned. $50.00 – 90.00. (Bottom) Fish pin, 2⅛". Mid-1960s to the early 1970s. Gold-tone scales with a ruby eye and small aurora borealis on the fins and tail. Lips are red enameling. $50.00 – 90.00.

(Top) 7⅛" This elegant silver-tone bracelet would be perfect for a winter bride. Pavè rhinestones in a swirl "s" design with faux pearls set between each. 1960s. Clasp is signed "TRIFARI." $90.00 – 130.00. (Bottom) 1960s unsigned bracelet. Ten links with four faux pearls glued in. Between each is a faux turquoise raised off of a wreath design with small faux pearls. Measures 7¼". $60.00 – 90.00.

79

Demi-parure clip earrings and choker necklace is made of gold tone with pavè rhinestone. The original Viva tag holds the earrings. Set in lions with emerald eyes. Earrings are on the original Brody's of Indiana, Pennsylvania, tag. Priced at $15.00. Lion measures 2½". Unsigned. Early to mid-1970s. $175.00 – 225.00.

Cute choker necklace with rhinestones set in the gold circle surrounding the lion. The lion's face is very detailed. Two heavy gold chains are used to suspend it. Unsigned. Early to mid-1970s. $150.00 – 190.00.

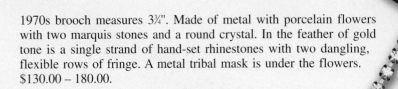

1970s brooch measures 3¾". Made of metal with porcelain flowers with two marquis stones and a round crystal. In the feather of gold tone is a single strand of hand-set rhinestones with two dangling, flexible rows of fringe. A metal tribal mask is under the flowers. $130.00 – 180.00.

Demi-parure brooch and clip earrings set. The pin measures 2¾" while the earrings are 1½". Both earrings are signed on the clip, "Astra," and on the lead "ORA." 1970s. For the set: $160.00 – 200.00.

Fab-o flower pin with two gold-tone flowers on one stem. The center of the flower is made up of dainty rhinestones. 1970s. Unsigned. $105.00 – 135.00.

Trifari gold-tone rose that measures 2½" long and is from the early 1960s. Ten small rhinestones are found in the center of the flower and a leaf over the stem to complete the single rose. $70.00 – 100.00.

LISNER pin 2½" from the mid-1950s to the early 1960s is weighted. Solid looking. Jagged leaf with a smaller jagged leaf on top. Gold tone. $75.00 – 105.00.

This antique gold-tone pendant converts to a brooch. Measures 2¼". From the 1960s. A vivid cameo design of three flowers. $50.00 – 80.00.

KRAMER clip earrings. 1¼". From the 1950s. Gold tone with white enameling. Small rhinestones scattered about. A white cabochon is set deep in the center. $75.00 – 115.00.

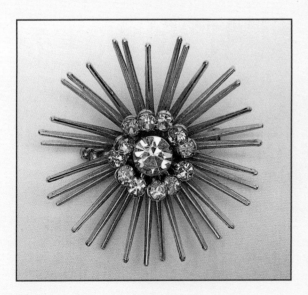

PAT 2066960 KRAMER 1950s pin. 2" in gold tone with three rows of jagged rods with a center of prong set stones. This one screams for attention. $95.00 – 145.00.

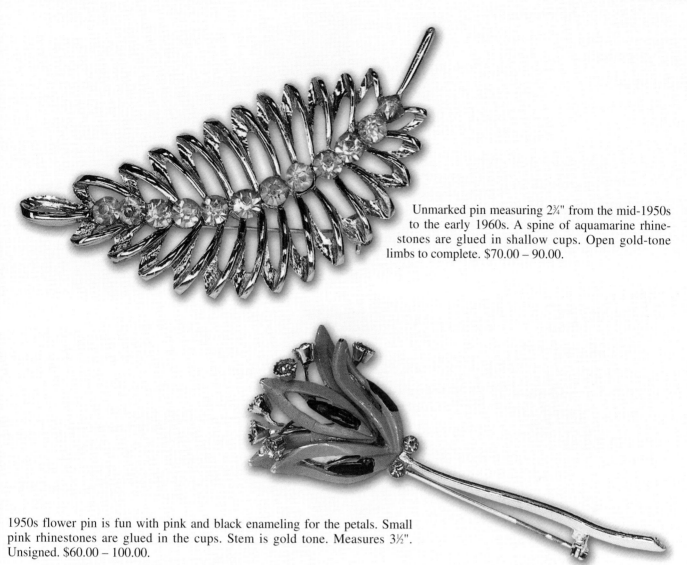

Unmarked pin measuring 2¾" from the mid-1950s to the early 1960s. A spine of aquamarine rhinestones are glued in shallow cups. Open gold-tone limbs to complete. $70.00 – 90.00.

1950s flower pin is fun with pink and black enameling for the petals. Small pink rhinestones are glued in the cups. Stem is gold tone. Measures 3½". Unsigned. $60.00 – 100.00.

Unsigned pin and clip earrings. 1960s. Gold tone in an open circle design with flowers and a lone leaf. Fuchsia stones are prong set in each flower and at the base of the leaf. Measures 1¾" and is unsigned. 1960s. $75.00 – 125.00.

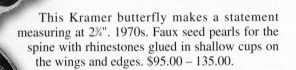

3½" Pastelli brooch. Haute couture of the 1960s. Gold tone over metal with a two fold jagged design over a spine. $90.00 – 130.00.

This Kramer butterfly makes a statement measuring at 2¾". 1970s. Faux seed pearls for the spine with rhinestones glued in shallow cups on the wings and edges. $95.00 – 135.00.

Lisner butterfly brooch is as mystical as the 1950s. Measures 2¼". Weighted. Two stones are missing on the spine. $70.00 – 100.00.

(Left) 1¾" Trifari feminine flowing brooch from the 1960s is done in gold tone. $80.00 – 130.00. (Right) Trifari gold-tone flower brooch from the late 1950s catches my eye. $60.00 – 80.00.

Majestic Monet rose pin measures 2¾" The clip earrings are ¾". All three pieces are signed. Quality from the 1970s. $110.00 – 130.00.

1970s rope circle pin with matching the clip earrings each with a faux pearl set on the inside. Each of the clip earrings is signed on the inside bottom of the clip, "pat pend." $85.00 – 115.00.

All three of these pieces are signed "Coro." The clip earrings and pin are in a raised jagged feather design. Earrings 1¼" and pin 3¾". 1950s to early 1960s. $105.00 – 125.00.

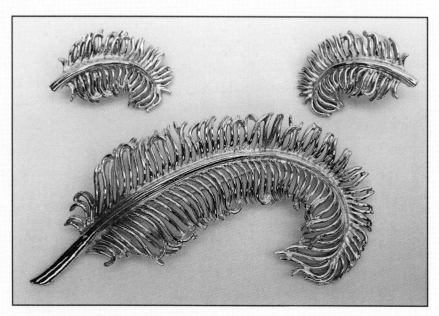

Six emerald-colored cabochons are set in brushed gold circles. Signed "DENICOLA." 6¾." 1950s. $140.00 – 170.00.

This 2½" gold-tone pin is from the 1970s. It has many amethyst, topaz, and ruby-colored, pear-shaped stones to make a lovely circle. $50.00 – 80.00.

Necklace and pierced earrings set. The original box was not photographed. Given to me by my mother-in-law. 25" long necklace. Signed "Jeanne" on the center of the necklace and each of the earrings. Rather flexible. $190.00 – 270.00.

4" Monet pin; original tag reads, "Monet $15.00," and on the other side, "Monet Cassandra 1741." 1970s to the early 1980s. $85.00 – 115.00.

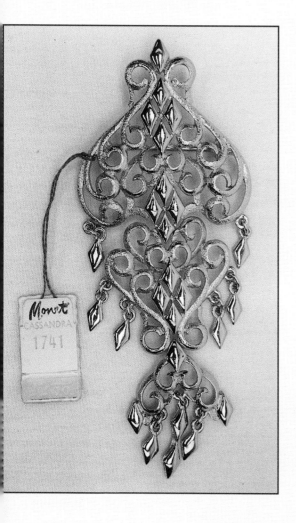

Lion on top of the pin. Very decorative and ornamental. 3¼". Unsigned. 1970s to the early 1980s. $95.00 – 135.00.

(Left) Monet circle pin with black enameling and small rhinestones in gold tone. 1960s to the early 1970s. 1½." $70.00 – 105.00. (Right) This Sarah Coventry circle pin is from the 1960s. 1¼." $60.00 – 90.00.

Lovely Monet pin with five flowers and open filigree work. 2¾." Late 1960s to the mid-1970s. $70.00 – 100.00.

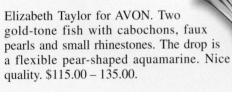

Hinged, grooved diamond design. Very weighted, cannot believe it isn't marked. 1970s. $75.00 – 105.00.

Elizabeth Taylor for AVON. Two gold-tone fish with cabochons, faux pearls and small rhinestones. The drop is a flexible pear-shaped aquamarine. Nice quality. $115.00 – 135.00.

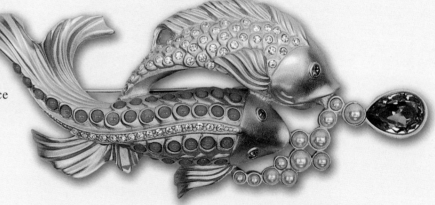

Shimmer in Silver Tone

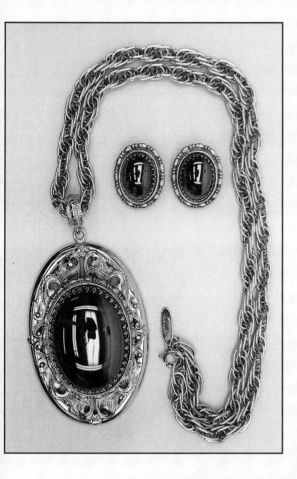

My hubby's number one pick. This shining necklace, with matching clip-on earrings, measures 13". The earrings are 1¾". Very heavy, very high quality workmanship. The cabochon center of the necklace is 3" wide by 2". The centers of the earrings are ¾". 1970s. Unsigned. $170.00 – 220.00.

Flower power! This set is comprised of a silver-tone necklace and matching screw-back earrings. At the center of this bulky chain, you will find a five-pointed flower that has an aqua center. The center glass is held by four prongs. Necklace chain measures 8¼", and the earrings are 1¼" wide. 1960s to the early 1970s. Unsigned. $110.00 – 160.00.

Four bulky links connect the three gold-tone plates with a gold bead cap. There is a safety catch on the clasp. This charming 7¾" bracelet from the 1960s is signed "MARINO." $90.00 – 120.00.

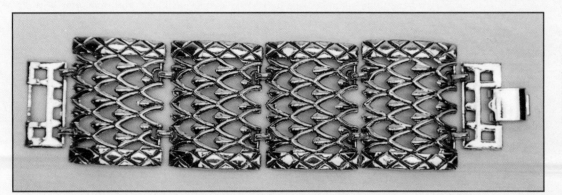

Hot and dazzling! This silver tone over copper-tone stunner is 7½" of four large filigree links. Unsigned. Late 1950s to mid-1960s. $70.00 – 100.00.

(Top) Two rows of six chain links are set off by three amethyst, emerald-shaped colored glass and three purple frosted, emerald-shaped cabochons. 6½" long. Unsigned, I'm surprised. Late 1950s. Silver-tone plating. $80.00 – 110.00. (Bottom) Seven silver-tone links with round rhinestones set in the middle. Six very small rhinestones at the ends. 7½" long. Early to mid-1960s. Unmarked. $80.00 – 110.00.

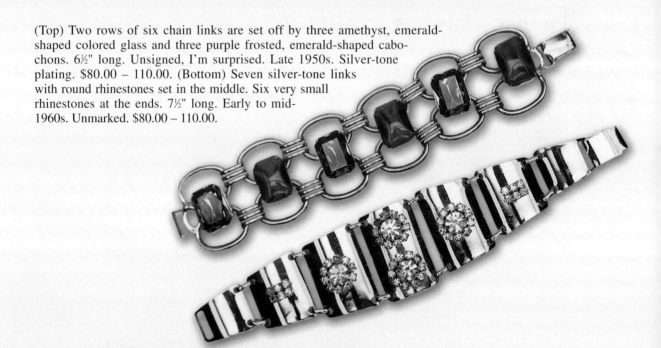

This very ornately detailed piece would make a perfect gift for a silver lover. The chunky links measure 2½" wide with applied detailing resembling a vine. Clasp has a safety catch. 6¾" long. Late 1950s. Signed "MARINO5" on the tip and lock of clasp. $95.00 – 135.00.

Superb silver tone over copper bracelet. Very heavy. Six 2½" links are bedazzled with raised spirals and a large center ball. Measures 7¼". Unmarked. Late 1950s to mid-1960s. $70.00 – 100.00.

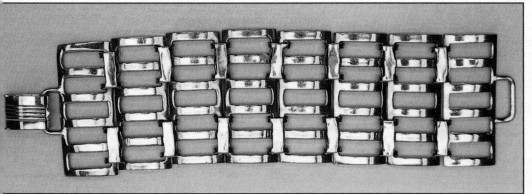

Fantastic fence-like bracelet from the late 1950s is unsigned. Eight 1¾" links total. Measures 6¼". Silver tone over metal. $65.00 – 85.00.

(Top) Sterling silver bracelet with six oval cabochons set in each link. Nice detailing. 6¾". The clasp is stamped "Sterling 925 Tax Co." Also, stamped "Mexico" on the back. 1950s. $130.00 – 180.00. (Bottom) Six square, light coral molded plastics are linked together forming this beauty. Safety chain on the clasp. Measures 7". 1950s. Unsigned. $120.00 – 160.00.

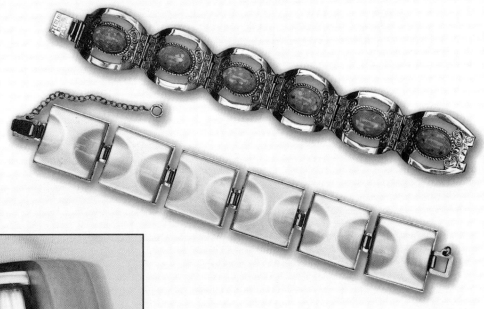

Simply stunning! This would be pretty with engraving also. A very tiny silver tone over metal bracelet to fit a small-boned wrist. Mid-1960s to mid-1970s. $60.00 – 80.00.

(Top) This bracelet is made of gold over brass. Bezel set, hand painted on porcelain. Designs of birds, flowers, deer, and water. Safety chain on the clasp. 7¼". 1900 to the 1920s. Unsigned. $120.00 – 150.00. (Bottom) Gold tone over brass. ½" lava cameos. Design in high carving or relief. 6¾". Clasp is stamped "083." Late 1800s to the mid-1900s. $180.00 – 250.00.

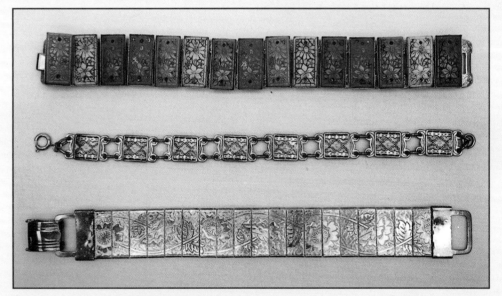

(Top) This silver-tone plated bracelet is bezel set with green, yellow, gray, and red shades. 7" long. Unmarked, which is hard to imagine! Looks like it could be from Mexico. 1930s. $95.00 – 145.00. (Center) Bracelet is gold wash over metal. Quite dainty. Eight squares of engraved tracks with flowers in the center. Squares are held by two links to each. Unsigned. 6½". 1930s. $75.00 – 105.00. (Bottom) Very thin bracelet. The back of the bracelet is gold mesh with the front clipped to the back. Gold flowers and green leaves are engraved on the links. 6¼". Unsigned. 1950s. $75.00 – 105.00.

(Top) Silver-tone plated bracelet with seven links held by two sets of two links. 7". 1950s. Unsigned. $95.00 – 125.00. (Bottom) Rather attractive gold tone over metal bracelet that is comprised of six links. 7¼". 1950s. $95.00 – 125.00.

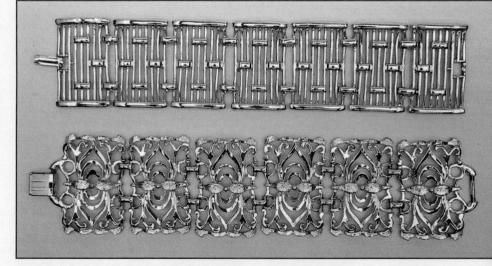

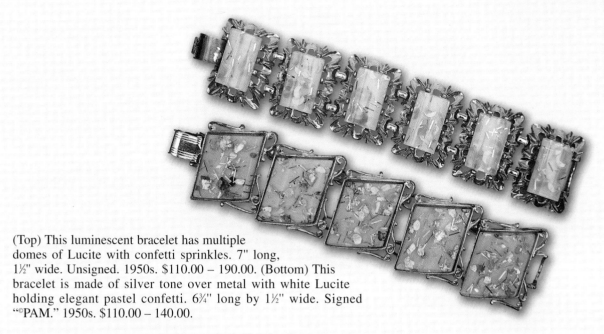

(Top) This luminescent bracelet has multiple domes of Lucite with confetti sprinkles. 7" long, 1½" wide. Unsigned. 1950s. $110.00 – 190.00. (Bottom) This bracelet is made of silver tone over metal with white Lucite holding elegant pastel confetti. 6¾" long by 1½" wide. Signed "©PAM." 1950s. $110.00 – 140.00.

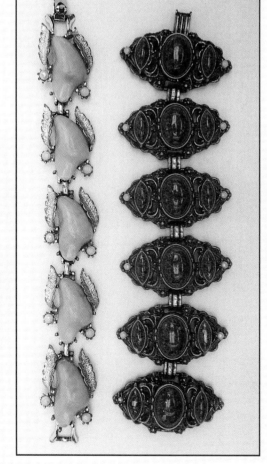

(Top) These clip earrings have gold sparkles with black and white flecks encased in plastic. 1¼". Unsigned. 1950s. $45.00 – 65.00. (Bottom) Antique silver tone with insets of 2" black onyx. 7¾" long by 2" wide. 1950s. Unsigned. Nice bracelet. $130.00 – 170.00.

(Left) This silver-tone bracelet has leaves with faux seed pearls on each side of the faux turquoise stones. 7¼" long. 1950s. Signed "Coro." 1950s. $120.00 – 160.00. (Right) This bracelet has an antique silver-tone look with two royal blue cabochons in marquee settings. 2" wide by 6¾". 1950s. Unsigned. $105.00 – 125.00.

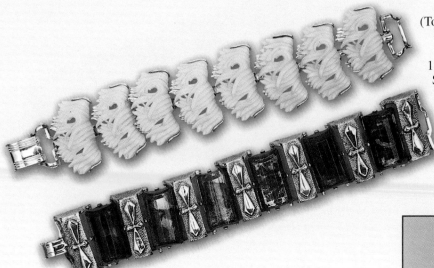

(Top) Daring signed STAR designer bracelet. One link holds these eight, pink, wispy plastic links in silver tone, together. 1950s. 7". $115.00 – 145.00. (Bottom) Seven silver-tone bars with an engraved design on each side of the amethyst dome. Closed backing. 6¾" long. Unsigned. 1950s. $110.00 – 150.00.

I love this one! Reminds me of Waylon Jennings and Jessie Coulter. Silver tone for sweet singing songbirds. Six faux turquoise on each side of the three rows of beads. The center is the top for the base of the 2¼" wide drop. Measures 15". 1970s. Unsigned. $175.00 – 225.00.

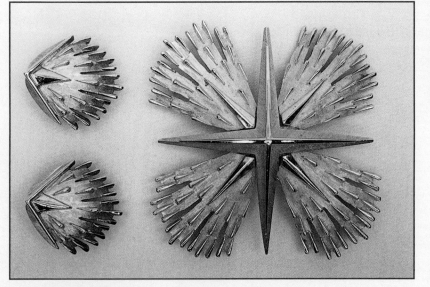

Demi-parure. Rhodium plated. The brooch is 2¾" and the earrings are 1". Signed "TRIFARI 1960s." Four large sections with a jagged design. In the center is the star. $135.00 – 165.00.

Marvelous swirl design with a faux center pearl. Rhodium. Measures 2½". 1960s. Brooch is signed "SARAH COV." $130.00 – 150.00. Earrings measure 1½" and are of a similar design. Great center knot. 1960s. $55.00 – 75.00.

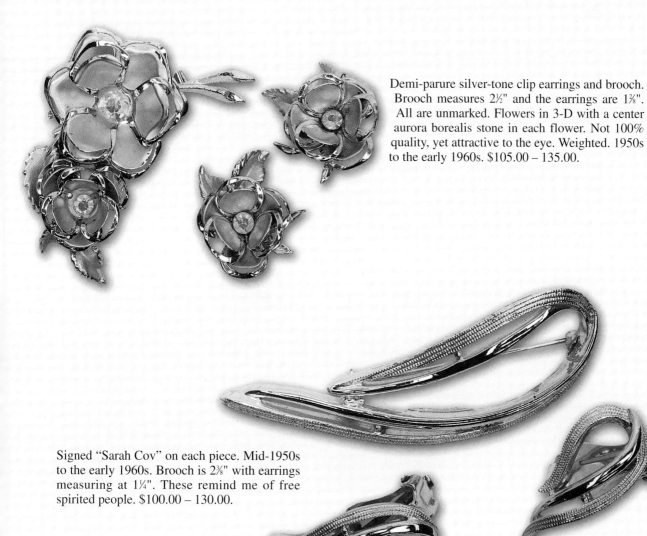

Demi-parure silver-tone clip earrings and brooch. Brooch measures 2½" and the earrings are 1⅜". All are unmarked. Flowers in 3-D with a center aurora borealis stone in each flower. Not 100% quality, yet attractive to the eye. Weighted. 1950s to the early 1960s. $105.00 – 135.00.

Signed "Sarah Cov" on each piece. Mid-1950s to the early 1960s. Brooch is 2⅜" with earrings measuring at 1¼". These remind me of free spirited people. $100.00 – 130.00.

(Top) Pin is weighted, unsigned, and measures 1¾". It is a design of graduated silver wire bars. Mid-1950s to the early 1960s. Attention getting. $90.00 – 120.00. (Bottom) Signed "STERLING" twice on each piece. Earrings are 1¼". Mid-1950s to the 1960s. $45.00 – 65.00.

This flower brooch is 3¼". Unsigned. Jagged petals off of two rows of flowers. A center of silver-tone beads. 1950s. Unsigned. $65.00 – 105.00.

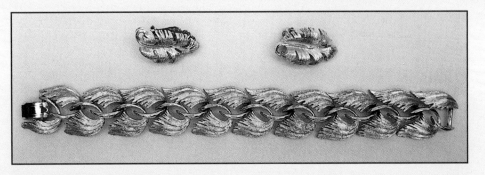

Signed "Lisner" on the clasp of the bracelet and the clips of the earrings. You are sure to look stunning in silver in this set. Late 1950s to the mid-1960s. Bracelet measures 7½" and the earrings are 1⅛". $120.00 – 160.00.

Bracelet is signed "Sarah Cov." Each of the clip earrings is signed "Sarah Cov." at the top and "pat pend Sarah Cov." on the bottom. Bracelet measures 7½", earrings measure ¾". Simple and statement making. You could dress this up or wear very casually. Four links connect the five links of the bezel set black plastic. If you are a lover of silver and black, this set has your name on it. $125.00 – 155.00.

(From top to bottom) (#1) Silver-tone bracelet, unsigned. 1970s. Measures 7". Holds one charm. $30.00 – 50.00. (#2) Weighted 7" silver-tone bracelet unmarked from the 1970s. Two rows of chains with round flat ¾" silver plates. $55.00 – 85.00. (#3) Bulky chain bracelet 7¼" long. Silver tone unmarked. 1950s. Mother Mary charm signed "1930 ITALY" with a cross and stars on the back of the charm. $80.00 – 120.00. (#4) 7¼" single chain silver-tone bracelet with one charm. Signed "A + Z STER-LING" on the clasp. $50.00 – 80.00.

Signed "Coro" on the clasp of this necklace. Measures 5½". Late 1950s to the early 1960s. A great heart design held by a silver link. 4¼" adjustable chain with a fish-hook clasp. $70.00 – 100.00.

The fish-hook clasp of this choker measuring 5¾" is signed "Coro." The adjustable chain is 3¾". Early 1950s to the late 1960s. $85.00 – 105.00.

Lightweight, insignificant necklace measures 11" and is signed "SAC" with a diamond surrounding the initials. 1960s. Simple round links designed with a round flat silver head with detailed flowers, and petals in an every-other pattern. $50.00 – 70.00.

Pendant in silver tone tha opens to hold a special pho on each side. I opened this ar was surprised to find the orig nal black and white picture of lady on the right side. Unmarke Early 1950s. This measures 1½ $100.00 – 130.00.

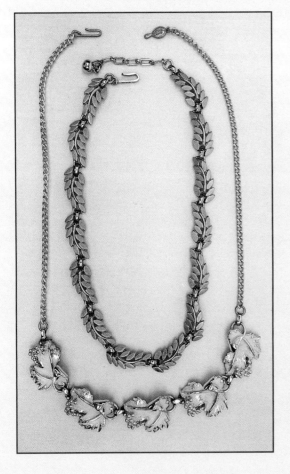

(Outer) Necklace signed "Sarah Cov" on the drop of the chain. Five leaves with silver berries and veins are detailed. They are held by a silver single link. Mea sures 7¼". Late 1950s to mid-1960s. $95.00 – 105.00. (Inner) TRIFARI signed choker. Mid-1950s. 2½" of adjustable chain with a fish-hook clasp and silver a the end. Fourteen sets of silver leaves with one silver-tone link holding each leaf. 6½" of leaves. $105.00 – 125.00.

(Left) Unsigned pin measuring 1½". 1950s. Silver tone. Enclosed back. Round stone set in dog teeth. $60.00 – 80.00. (Right) Unsigned pin measuring 1½". Abalone is open back. Front abalone is held in place with six prongs. Enclosed in a swirl design. Late 1950s. $115.00 – 135.00.

(Top) Clip earrings, each signed "STERLING RS DENMARK." 1950s. Measures 1⅛". $45.00 – 75.00. (Bottom) Brooch that converts to a pendant. Early 1950s. Signed "STERLING AP TAZCC 325." Measures 1¾" in a triangle design with tiger's eye and an abalone owl. A star of abalone on the bottom right. $130.00 – 150.00.

This pin, signed "STERLING UL MEXICO 825," is sure to be a wow-er for spring break in MEXICO! Measures 1½". One of the screw-back earrings has the same signature. Earrings each measure 1". Abalone and silver. 1950s. $130.00 – 160.00.

Bracelet measuring 7¼" signed "EM MEXICO TAM" on the clasp. Five links of silver beaded squares holding 1⅛" of green molded plastic. 1950s. $110.00 – 150.00.

(Left) Primitive brooch of the 1930s. Measures 3". Silver over metal; crudely done. The center is a prong-set amethyst. Seven rhinestones are missing around the flower. Leaves also have missing rhinestones. They were glued in. $40.00 – 70.00. (Right) A burst of rays from the silver-tone beauty with a center ocean blue stone that is glued in. Very heavy. Early 1940s. $75.00 – 95.00.

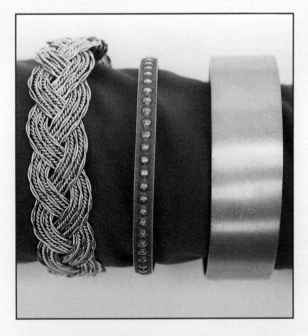

(Left) Cuff bracelet from the 1950s. Unsigned. Twisted rope design in silver. Weighty. $50.00 – 70.00. (Center) Signed "Sterling" from the 1950s. Raised center beads on the bracelet. Simple in style. Fits a very small wrist. $40.00 – 60.00. (Right) Cuff bracelet signed "PEWTER BDA" from the 1950s. $90.00 – 120.00.

Pin is signed "SIAM STERLING" and measures 2½". Earrings measure 1¼". Each of the earrings is signed "SIAM STERLING." 1950s. As always, nice detailing on SIAM STERLING. $125.00 – 155.00.

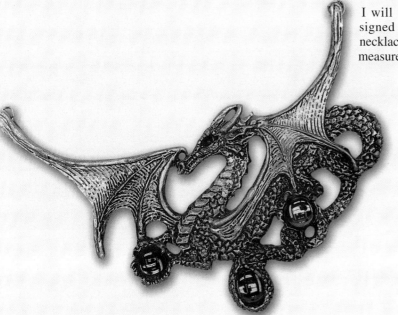

I will say this is one that I despise. This necklace is signed "Fellowship Foundry 19 OHARE." Silver-tone necklace with three molded blue purple stones. The center measures 5½" and the chain is 8½". I cannot assign a value.

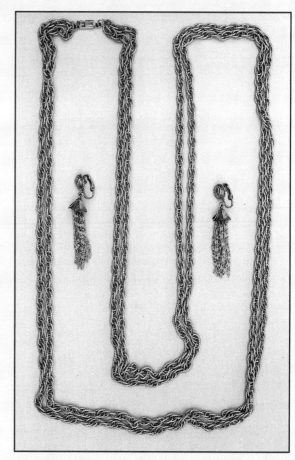

(Outer) Necklace. Two silver-tone links connect this long strand to be worn knotted. It measures 27¼" long, so how else would it be worn? Signed on the clasp, "MADE IN WEST GERMANY." Late 1940s to the early 1950s. $90.00 – 120.00. (Center) Clip earrings. Thirteen chains dangle from the silver-tone tassel drop. 2½" long. Late 1940s. $40.00 – 70.00.

(Left) Necklace. Sixteen chains or candles as the saying may go. They are in groups of four and drop from silver-tone hooks. Great colors for the winter holidays. Silver-tone clasp is unsigned but shows great detail. Measures 15½" for the long and 12" for the short set. $55.00 – 105.00. (Right) Necklace unsigned. Done in silver tone chains, links, and a staple design in two sets of three with a center rope, totaling seven chains. 1970s. Clasp is ¾" with open filigree design. $55.00 – 105.00.

(Top left) Clip earrings signed "STERLING CORO." 1940s. Two leaves with a rose. $55.00 – 95.00. (Top right) Screw earrings. Metal flowers each with a center rhinestone. $40.00 – 50.00. (#2 and #3) Seeing double! Bracelets 7⅛" of metal. Two leaves hold a flower with a center rhinestone. Done in six flowers linked by 12 metal ring links. $60.00 – 120.00. (#4) Sterling signed pin. 1¾". Three metal with a center rhinestone on a single vine with four leaves. $50.00 – 80.00. (#5) Four-rose circle pin measuring 1¾". Rose has a center rhinestone. Heavy. $50.00 – 80.00. (Bottom) Necklace, 6" of flowers, 9½" of chain. Five metal flowers are set on top of two leaves with a center rhinestone. $100.00 – 140.00.

Matching clip earrings, bracelet, and necklace. The necklace is signed twice on each clasp. Each of the clip earrings is signed, and the clasp on the bracelet is signed "TRIFARI." 1950s. Silver tone in style of the 1950s. The necklace measures 10½" closed. Late 1950s. $115.00 – 145.00.

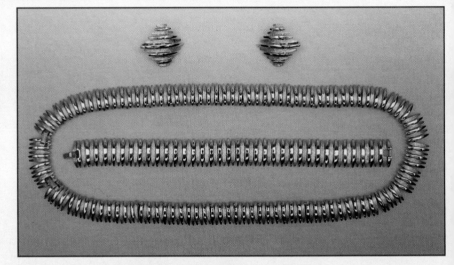

(Outer) Signed Lisner necklace in silver tone. Done in a leaf pattern. Heavy 3¾" adjustable chain with a ball drop. (Center) Clip earrings signed "TRIFARI." Each one has a simple silver-tone leaf. 1950s. For the set: $50.00 – 80.00.

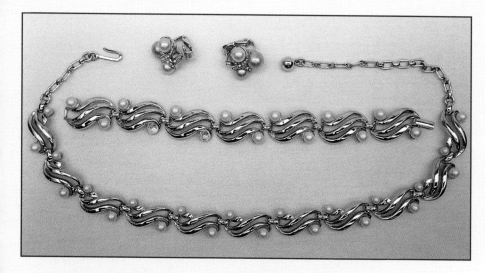

(Top) Clip earrings, signed "TRIFARI" with three pearls in a figure eight pattern of paste rhinestones from the 1950s. $50.00 – 80.00. (Bottom) Demi-parure bracelet signed "TRIFARI" on clasp with the necklace being signed on the fish-hook clasp. The bracelet measures 7" and has two small pearls missing. The necklace measures 6" of adjustable chain with a silver ball to drop. Eleven links in two rows with a small pearl at each end held by a single silver link. 1950s. For the set: $105.00 – 145.00.

(Top) Lisner screw-on earrings in silver tone. From the 1950s. $40.00 – 60.00. (Bottom) Monet clip earrings. ¾". From the 1950s to the early 1960s. $40.00 – 60.00.

Coro, silver-tone pin from the 1950s. 1¾" of two rows of silver tone spun in a flower design with a raised center. $50.00 – 70.00.

(Top) STAR silver tone screw-on earrings. 1960s. 1". $35.00 – 65.00. (Bottom) Sarah Coventry clip earrings. 1¼". 1960s. $40.00 – 60.00.

(Top) Trifari clip earrings. Silver-tone jagged edges with a tulip shape. 1960s. $35.00 – 65.00. (Bottom) Trifari clip earrings in silver tone from the 1960s. A leaf borders the silver beaded center. $35.00 – 65.00.

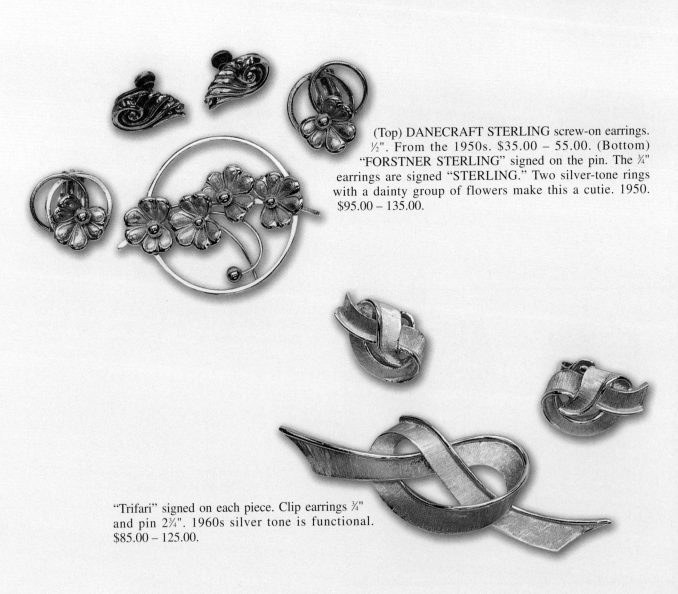

(Top) DANECRAFT STERLING screw-on earrings. ½". From the 1950s. $35.00 – 55.00. (Bottom) "FORSTNER STERLING" signed on the pin. The ¾" earrings are signed "STERLING." Two silver-tone rings with a dainty group of flowers make this a cutie. 1950. $95.00 – 135.00.

"Trifari" signed on each piece. Clip earrings ¾" and pin 2¾". 1960s silver tone is functional. $85.00 – 125.00.

(Top) Beau Sterling four leaf clover pin with a center faux pearl set on sprigs of silver. 1950s. 2½". $60.00 – 90.00. (Bottom) 1½" filigree flower pin from the 1950s. Unsigned. $45.00 – 65.00.

Unsigned pin from the 1950s. Two sizes of three leaves that are raised. Tips are sharp. Weighted. 2⅛". $65.00 – 95.00.

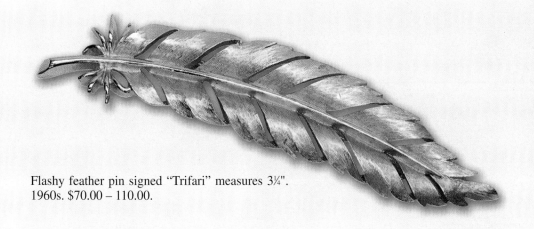

Flashy feather pin signed "Trifari" measures 3¼". 1960s. $70.00 – 110.00.

(Outer) Sterling screw-on earrings, 1" with a single prong-set rhinestone. 1960s. $35.00 – 55.00. (Inner) Delicate 1950s silver-tone pin is 1½" with three faux pearls set off of the open filigree leaves. $105.00 – 115.00.

Flower brooch is 3¼" with 1½" clip earrings. These bright starbursts have five petals, each with a center aurora borealis. Late 1950s to the mid-1960s. $105.00 – 125.00.

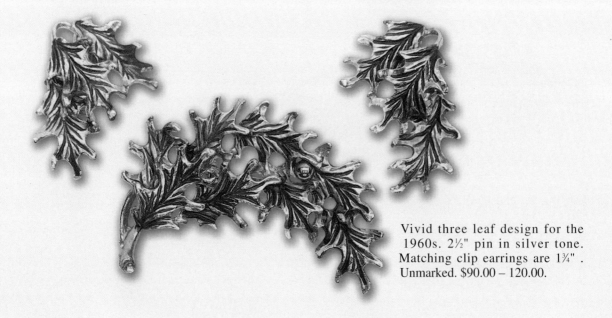

Vivid three leaf design for the 1960s. 2½" pin in silver tone. Matching clip earrings are 1¾". Unmarked. $90.00 – 120.00.

Bow-wow! Bow-wow! for the pretty poodle sweater pins. Complete with onyx eyes. 1950s. Unmarked. $55.00 – 85.00.

(Left) SANCREST M 1970s turquoise necklace. Measures 1¼" . $100.00 – 120.00. (Right) Unsigned cross. 2½" with a chain of 11½". 1970s. $115.00 – 145.00.

1950s. 2⅛" weighted leaf pin with a center silver ball with matching clip earrings. Nice workmanship for an unsigned set. $110.00 – 140.00.

Rhinestones, Rhinestones, Rhinestones

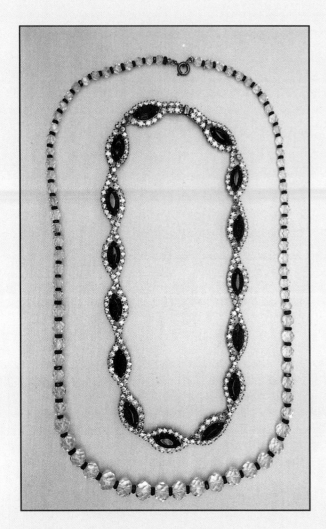

(Outer) The string of this necklace is discolored and shows through two of the crystals. Glass crystals are strung on a heavy string with spacers between each crystal. 12¼". Late 1920s to the mid-1930s. Unsigned. $90.00 – 130.00. (Inner) Small chaton-cut, marquee-shaped rhinestones encase black marquee-cut glass. 17" long. Unsigned. Late 1940s to the early 1950s. $120.00 – 150.00.

(Left) Clip earrings. Two black beads/balls dangle from the dainty gold chain with prong-set faux onyx. 2¼". Unsigned. Early 1960s. $40.00 – 70.00. (Right) Clip earrings. Clip of small rhinestones with large center stone. One braided chain with small rhinestones around the braid. 2½". Unmarked. Early 1960s. $70.00 – 100.00.

(Center) Clip earrings. 3-D pair of small rhinestones in between a pair of black beads create a cross of rhinestones. Signed "Vogue." Mid- to late 1960s. $50.00 – 90.00. (Outer) Choker. Fish-hook clasp with two black beads with a rhinestone spacer. 6½". Looks like Vogue. Mid- to late 1960s. $60.00 – 100.00.

This precious peridot center stone is sure to pop a few eyes. The stone is set in a thick gold ring. Nice filigree work for the base of this beauty. Stone is open backed. 1950s. Measures 2½". Unsigned. $130.00 – 160.00.

Three aurora borealis rhinestones outline this pin. Eight light green, pear-shaped stones are set on gold tone, open backing. A nicely crafted piece! Late 1940s to the mid-1950s. 2" wide. Unsigned. $100.00 – 130.00.

August and November. These two colors absolutely glow together! Brooch measures 2¼". Chaton-cut citrines are set on a gold-tone backing and the peridot tapered baguettes highlight this piece. Late 1940s to the mid-1950s. Unsigned. $110.00 – 130.00.

Buzzing birds! Aqua and peridot marquee-shaped stones with royal blue rhinestones form a bird-like figure. A pear-shaped peridot stone is used for the head. 2¼" wide. Unsigned. 1940s to the mid-1950s. $100.00 – 130.00.

A gorgeous flower, indeed! Emerald and citrine-colored marquees create petals and leaves on this pretty flower. The stem is a delicate gold sprig. 3" long. Gold-tone plating. Early 1950s. $90.00 – 110.00.

(Left) A closed backing completes the oval emerald-colored stone set in the middle of this pin. Faux seed pearls are glued around the center. The framing is gold tone with four heart shapes and four small emerald-colored rhinestones. Early 1950s. Signed "Coro." $45.00 – 65.00. (Center) This unsigned butterfly pin has wings made of jadeite. Early 1950s. $40.00 – 60.00. (Right) Rather simple, rather eye catching. Foiled back oval emerald stone set in a whimsical shape. Early 1950s. $40.00 – 60.00.

Luscious leaves! This gold-tone pin has six large aurora borealis stones glued in to shallow cups; the other marquee-shaped leaves are made of small pavè rhinestones. Late 1940s to the early 1950s. Measures 2¾". Unmarked. $75.00 – 100.00.

Holy horseshoe! Frosty, light blue, marquee-shaped cabochons are set in a horseshoe style pin. Dark blue small, round chaton cut stones rim the center. The marquee stones are open backed. Hand set on silver tone. 2" wide by 2¼" long. Unsigned. 1940s. $70.00 – 100.00.

Splendid sticks of light brown and aurora borealis, chaton-cut stones make up this late 1940s KRAMER pin. Prong set; gold-tone plating. $90.00 – 130.00.

Brilliantly bold brooch! This heavyweight has five large ocean blue rhinestones with five royal blue round stones separating the larger ones. To finish the brooch, a filigree finish and sparkling center stones. All stones handset; silver-tone plating. 1940s. 2¼" long. Unsigned. $90.00 – 120.00.

Banging on the banjo brooch! All stones are set on gold-tone plating by hand. The 3-D look completes the base of the banjo. Aurora borealis stones are used in place of the strings. 2½" long. Unsigned. Early to mid-1950s. $65.00 – 105.00.

Striking! Bam! This catches the eye and causes a smile. Demi-parure clip earrings and pin. Silver-tone plating; hand-set stones. All open backing. Steel blue marquees with two large emerald-shaped stones in the center and offset by 25 small aurora borealis stones. Brooch measures 3" across; earrings 1¼" long. Unmarked, a certain surprise to me. Late 1940s. For the set: $120.00 – 150.00.

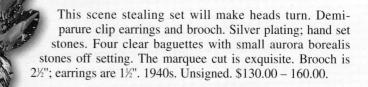

This scene stealing set will make heads turn. Demi-parure clip earrings and brooch. Silver plating; hand set stones. Four clear baguettes with small aurora borealis stones off setting. The marquee cut is exquisite. Brooch is 2½"; earrings are 1½". 1940s. Unsigned. $130.00 – 160.00.

An amalgam of colors! Demi-parure clip earrings and brooch. Plating is gold wash over metal; stones are set. Multi-colored cabochons and glass pieces are set on an open backing. Brooch measures 2½". Earrings are 1¼". Early 1950s. Unsigned. $110.00 – 140.00.

This pin and clip earrings demi-parure will have you mooning, or rather swooning, over the wonderful, lustrous pavè citrines and gray rhinestones which are set in a half-moon shape. Plating is gold filigree. Early 1950s. 2¼" wide and the earrings are 1". "KARU Duke Inc." $160.00 – 180.00.

(Left) Aloha, pineapple lovers! I love this pin! It can also be worn as a pendant. Gold-tone plating; 1¾" in length. Citrine-colored glass topped with a golden flower. The facets are highly detailed. Late 1950s to the early 1960s. Signed "Sarah Cov." $55.00 – 85.00. (Right) Fabulous flower-shaped pin. This is no Brown-eyed Susan. Gold-tone plating; set prong. 1¾" wide and ¾" long. Unmarked, though it looks like Coro. Late 1940s to the early 1950s. $45.00 – 65.00.

(Top) Cute clips. Silver-tone plated; set prongs. Three deep blue marquees border three aqua-colored flowers. 1". Unsigned. 1940s to 1950s. $55.00 – 75.00. (Bottom) Clip earrings. Silver-tone plating; prong set. The centers are aurora borealis stones surrounded by dark blue raised stones and other aurora borealis. Measure ¾". Unsigned. 1940s to the 1950s. $45.00 – 65.00.

Pretty, precious pin and comfortable clip-on earrings. The really red round stones and aurora borealis stones are set on a gold-tone plating. The earrings match the pin with their five, small, flexible beads. 1940s to the 1950s. Each of the earrings is signed "Weiss." For the set: $120.00 – 160.00.

(Left) No fuss filigree! The work is great, and not too over done. Six small round aurora borealis stones separate the six ruby-colored marquees. A round stone is in the center. 1950s. Unsigned. 2¼". Gold-tone plating. $50.00 – 70.00. (Right) Perfect pin has gold washing over metal plating. Aurora borealis stones are glued in shallow cups. Lovely contrasts of reds and blues. 1½". 1940s era. Unsigned. $45.00 – 55.00.

Demi-parure bracelet and clip earrings. Gold-tone plating. This banging bracelet has ovular topaz-colored stones and dogtooth style set blue topaz chatons. Earrings measure 1" and the bracelet measures 6½". Late 1940s to the early 1950s. Unsigned. $95.00 – 115.00.

Necklace with many niceties. Silver tone, vine-like necklace with a mix of glued pearls and stems. The lovely blue rhinestones absolutely glisten. Fish-hook clasp to close. 7½". From the 1950s. Signed "©Listner." $65.00 – 95.00.

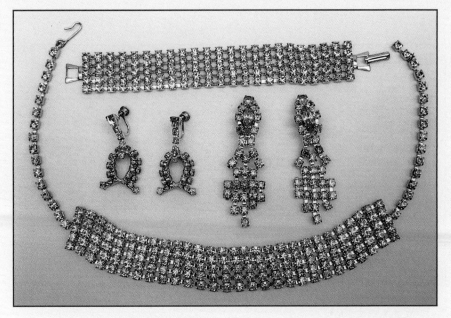

All pieces from the late 1940s to the 1950s. Grouping consists of all unsigned pieces. A bracelet, a set of screw-back earrings, a set of clip-on earrings, and a necklace. (Bracelet) Five rows of sparkling hand-set aquamarine chaton cut stones. Bracelet measures 5¾". $60.00 – 80.00. (Screw backs, left) Measure 1¼" with alarmingly beautiful stones. $45.00 – 50.00. (Clip earrings, right) Measure 2½" and are breathtaking. $60.00 – 65.00. (Necklace) Measures 6¾" and is made up of five rows of stones with 3¾" of a single strand to lead to a fish-hook closure. $90.00 – 120.00.

(Top) Bracelet is gold tone. Two dashing strands of chaton-cut stones with three graduated stones on each side of the center stone. Measures 7" long. Unsigned. From the 1950s. $45.00 – 60.00. (Bottom) Gold-tone choker with eight aurora borealis flowers separated by nine aurora borealis stones. Center strand 6¾", other strand 5½", and the fish-hook clasp strand 3". From the 1940s. Unsigned. $65.00 – 95.00.

Bountiful brooch of gold wash over metal with four faux pearls and eight pear-shaped faux marbleized turquoise cabochons and an oval center to finish. Converts to a pendant. Late 1950s to the 1960s. Signed "©Sarah Cov." $65.00 – 85.00.

Sleek and chic! Marquees entwine with chaton-cut, clear rhinestones. Measures 3". From the 1940s to the 1950s. Unsigned. Resembles a music clef. $70.00 – 90.00.

(Left) This beautiful pin converts to a pendant. Six blue emerald-colored flowers have blue rhinestone centers. Measures 1½". From the early Avon collection. $30.00 – 40.00. (Right) Five blue enameled flowers with enameled green leaves on gold tone. A dogtooth pronging holds the amethyst and aqua-colored stones. Unsigned. Measures 2" long and is from the 1950s era. $35.00 – 55.00.

(Left) Bezel-set lined star. The star is open backed. Very simple filigree with a leaf to each side of the silver tone. Measures 1¼" and is from the 1960s. Unsigned. $30.00 – 40.00. (Right) The set center royal blue rhinestone is encompassed by a row of faux seed pearls and smaller royal rhinestones. Signed "Coro" on the top and under the pin. Early 1950s and measures 1¼" long. $40.00 – 70.00.

Grab your peanuts; it's time for the Scatter Pin Circus! (Top) Small men are enameled on a gold-tone plating. They have a hat, bow, arms, and feet; painted faux pearl face. Early 1950s. Measures 1½" long. Unsigned. $15.00 – 25.00. (Bottom) Pavè rhinestones for the back with three red cabochons and emerald rhinestones for the eyes. The under shell is silver tone with the limbs, head, and tail, in gold tone. Late 1950s to the 1960s. 1¾" long. Unsigned. $25.00 – 35.00.

Vivid silver-tone bow brooch with a row of baguettes and round rhinestones. The baguettes are prong set and the round stones are glued. Measures 2½". 1950s. Signed "Sterling." $95.00 – 135.00.

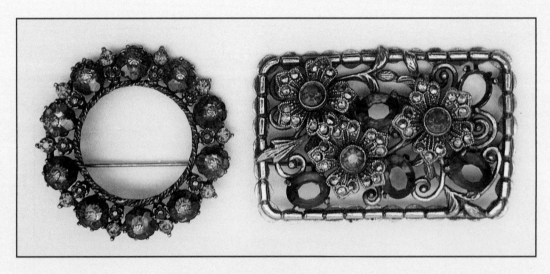

(Left) Crude craftsmanship. This unmarked pin has four emerald-colored stones with three flowers done in marquisate and an open stone in the center. Measures 2½" long and is from the late 1950s. $45.00 – 75.00. (Right) A circle pin with small metal flowers tipped off with small emerald rhinestones. Every other flower has a large flower with a silver-tone center. Measures 1½" and is from the 1950s. "©Weiss." $50.00 – 80.00.

Sophisticated circle burst brooch with three varied sizes of stones set in gold toning. 1¾" diameter. Unsigned. 1950s. $110.00 – 150.00.

This is a pin any jewelry lover would simply go gaga for! Measures 2½" in length. The glued rhinestones are in the shape of marquees, baguettes, and chaton cuts. Three-leaved beauty! 1950s. Signed "PELL." $120.00 – 160.00.

Hats off to this brooch! Measures 2¾" in length. Chaton-cut rhinestones are handset with baguettes to finish. Unmarked. Late 1950s to the mid-1960s. $120.00 – 150.00.

A flowery brooch of marquees and hoops of chaton-cut rhinestones to complete the bouquet. 3-D. ¼" high and 2¾" long. 1950s. Unsigned. $120.00 – 150.00.

(Left) Chaton-cut rhinestones are glued in four rows with a center stone glued into a shallow cup. Because all the stones are of the same enormity, this makes the brooch rather striking. 1¾" diameter. 1940s to the 1950s. Unsigned. $110.00 – 130.00. (Right) Chaton, baguette, and emerald-cut rhinestone in a swirl design. The center is a single, lone rhinestone. Measures 1¾" and is ½" high. Unsigned. Late 1940s to the early 1950s. $120.00 – 150.00.

Great for a Pittsburgh Steelers fan! Luscious black and yellow rhinestones make this pin striking. The leaves have three rows per leaf of yellow rhinestones; the center stem is finished with black baguettes, topped off by a black marquee. Measures 2¾". Unmarked, I'm shocked. 1950s. $120.00 – 150.00.

Festive fall colors in topaz, peridot, and amber dominate the necklace. The center yellow chaton-cut stone measures 1". The chain is 9" to the drop, which is 5¾" long and 2" wide. Signed "Avon" on the chain's clasp hook. 1980s. $90.00 – 120.00.

Decorative brooch that converts to a pendant. Silver tone over metal plating. Marquees, diamonds, pears, and round rhinestones finish this hefty beauty. Marquee-cut stones are in clear and aurora borealis with gray-colored rhinestones. Loads of depth in this piece. Signed "Made in Austria." 1950s. $140.00 – 190.00.

Bright belt buckle. My mother wears this on a herringbone chain, as a necklace. This weighty buckle is 3¼" long and 2" wide. ¾" yellow, oval stones with chaton-cut rhinestones make up this closed-back buckle. Late 1950s to the early 1960s. Unsigned. $180.00 – 250.00.

Very three dimensional. Round gray stones, light gray marquees, brown oval stones, and a center brown marquee-cut stone complete this heavy brooch. 2" in diameter. Unmarked. Late 1940s to the early 1950s. $140.00 – 190.00.

This shocking gold tone plated brooch converts to a pendant. All stones are set by hand. Oval stones abound in light gray shades and salmon shades. The center crystal is surrounded by 12 round, same shaded stones. Measures 2" by 2". Signed "Schreiner of New York." Late 1940s to the early 1950s. $150.00 – 200.00.

Super fly scatter pins composed of eight pear-shaped topazes. The topazes rise to the round center stone. Measures 1¼". Signed "Weiss Co." 1940s to the 1950s. For the pair: $90.00 – 140.00.

Precious pin and clip earrings set. For the pin: light yellow, citrine, and aurora borealis round stones hold three mobile fringes. The fringes are made of light yellow and aurora borealis stones. The large round stones at the top are open backed. The stones in both the earrings and the pin are set by hand on gold tone. Pin measures 2½"; earrings 1". Unsigned. 1940s to the 1950s. For the set: $145.00 – 185.00.

(Left) This gold-tone pin converts to a pendant. Two sizes of aurora borealis rhinestones with the larger stone encompassing two rows of smaller stones. Very fun! 2¼". Unsigned. Late 1940s to the mid-1950s. $110.00 – 150.00. (Right) Great detailing for this brooch. Larger stones are used to make it extra aesthetically pleasing. Marquees and pears on open backing; gray and clears on closed. Three aurora borealis stones scattered throughout unevenly. Late 1940s to the mid-1950s. 2¾". Unsigned. $130.00 – 180.00.

Fantastic necklace and clip earrings. Five dark colored, topaz-shaped stones with three forming a fringe drop. The drops are surrounded by light topaz-colored, chaton-cut rhinestones. One pear-shaped stone per side. A fish-hook clasp is used to close. Matching clip earrings. 8" necklace; 1¼" earrings. Unsigned. Late 1940s to the mid-1950s. Unsigned. For the set: $185.00 – 225.00.

Elaborate necklace and screw-on earrings set. Chaton cut, topaz-colored stones with a fringe of peridot and topaz-colored stones. Necklace 8½"; earrings 1½". 1940s to the 1950s. Unsigned. For the set: $160.00 – 200.00.

Three-piece parure necklace, earrings, and bracelet. Silver-tone plating. 1940s to the early 1950s. One of a kind! $155.00 – 195.00.

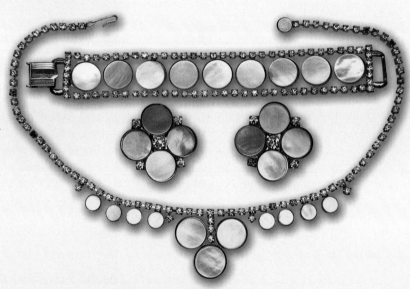

Vibrant necklace! This high quality necklace is comprised of round and oval stones which are all open backed. The fish-hook clasp measures 5¾" and is made of oval stones with four round stones. Necklace is 14½". Unsigned. Early to mid-1950s. $125.00 – 165.00.

Fit for the neck of a princess. This silver-tone plated necklace has a fish-hook clasp. A single strand of rhinestones with a drop. Three rows of rhinestones hug three marquees. On each side is an emerald center. Measures 6⅛". 1940s to the 1950s. Unsigned. $125.00 – 155.00.

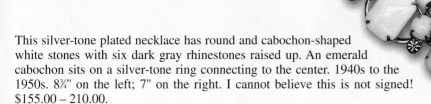

This silver-tone plated necklace has round and cabochon-shaped white stones with six dark gray rhinestones raised up. An emerald cabochon sits on a silver-tone ring connecting to the center. 1940s to the 1950s. 8¾" on the left; 7" on the right. I cannot believe this is not signed! $155.00 – 210.00.

Magnificent choker that is fit for a queen. Six rows of chaton-cut rhinestones connect to five rows of chaton-cut rhinestones with a giant, gray, oval center. Total of 14½". Fish-hook clasp. Unsigned. 1950s. $150.00 – 200.00.

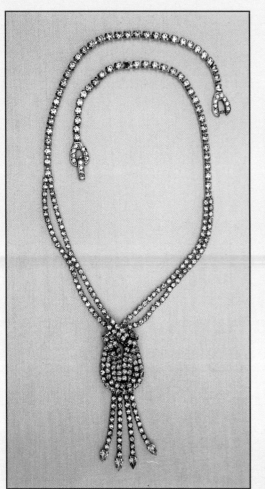

Kramer necklace which is simply elegant. A single strand of rhinestones with side fringing is simply smashing. Love the clasp which is rhodium and glued-in rhinestones. One stone is missing towards the top. Late 1940s to the mid-1950s. 11½". $120.00 – 160.00.

This ultra-feminine necklace has a single strand of rhinestones with three sides of fringe dropping to showcase a magnificent center of rhinestones. Late 1940s to the early 1950s. 10". $145.00 – 200.00.

Brilliant butterfly brooch! It can fly into my house any day. The outline base is sterling with a raised body. Measures 2½" in the center. Signed "Sterling." 1940s. $120.00 – 170.00.

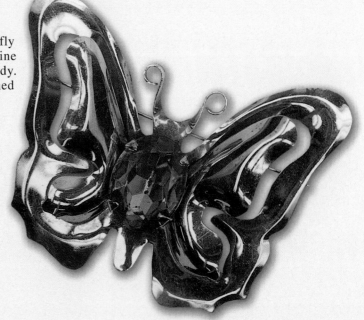

Attractive necklace and screw-back earrings set. Silver chain attaches the center attraction of royal blue marquees and aqua baguettes. Signed "Duane" on each earring. Also signed on the end of the silver chain. Mid-1950s to the 1960s. Necklace is 6¾" with a 4½" adjustable chain. $120.00 – 150.00.

Fabulous CoroCraft flower bouquet. Very weighty. Fourteen ocean blue marquees are glued in deep cups with two tiny rhinestones between the three marquees. 2¼" long. 1950s. $75.00 – 125.00.

Pin and screw-on earrings set. Aqua-colored baguettes circle the rhinestones; very simply done, excellent quality. 1½" in diameter. Signed "Sterling" on each of the earrings and the pin is signed "CA." Late 1950s to the 1960s. For the set: $85.00 – 115.00.

This pin is made of silver toning over white metal. Eight aurora borealis rhinestones are glued in deep between. A sort of silver, peas in a pod style. 2½" long. 1950s to the 1960s. Looks like ART. $50.00 – 70.00.

(Top) Clip-on rhinestone earrings. Two marquees fringe from the round rhinestones. Very flexible. Unsigned. 1950s. $55.00 – 75.00. (Bottom) Rhinestone earrings with round, chaton-cut rhinestones. A burst of three sizes of quality stones. 1". Unsigned. 1950s. $60.00 – 80.00.

Set, chaton-cut rhinestones of two sizes are in a circle. The back of the pin has patina. 1¼" diameter. Signed "Austria." 1940s. $60.00 – 90.00.

(Left) Five large pear-shaped stones with a round rhinestone for the center to bedazzle these clip-on earrings. Late 1940s to the 1950s era. 1⅛". Signed "Weiss." $80.00 – 120.00. (Center) Silver-tone plated clip-on earrings that measure 1⅛". Large square, emerald, pear, and small round rhinestones make up these earrings. Signed "Weiss." Late 1940s to the 1950s. $80.00 – 120.00. (Right) Two large marquee-cut stones with smaller marquees surround a round rhinestone. Late 1940s to the 1950s. Signed "Weiss." 1¼". $80.00 – 120.00.

(Top) This rhodium plated bracelet has two rows of chaton-cut rhinestones with a clasp made from two rhinestones. Late 1940s to the 1950s. $115.00 – 145.00. (Center) This silver-tone plated bracelet simply sparkles with its baguettes. But the central attraction of this bracelet are the chaton-cut rhinestones attached to each side. Measures 6½". Late 1940s to the 1950s. Signed "Weiss." $110.00 – 140.00. (Bottom) This silver-tone plated bracelet has two rows of small, quality aurora borealis rhinestones. Measures 7⅛". Signed "Weiss." Late 1940s to the 1950s. $115.00 – 145.00.

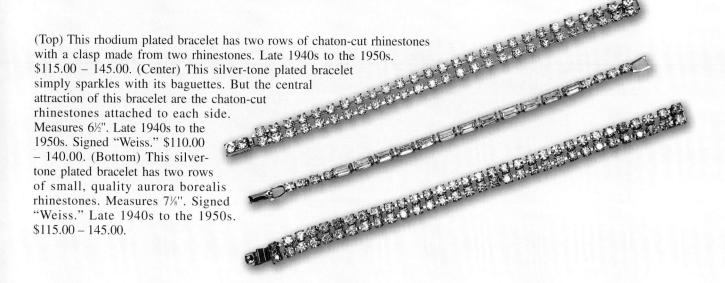

Choker/necklace with a matching bracelet. Emeralds abound in this set. This can be a dressed up or dressed down look. Necklace measures 14¼"; bracelet is 6¾". Unsigned. Late 1940s to the 1950s. For the set: $135.00 – 175.00.

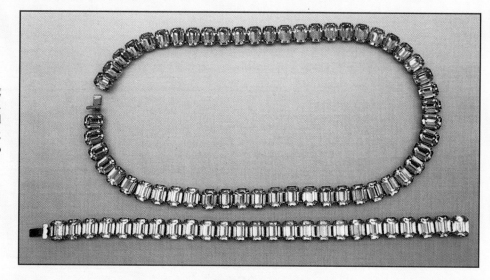

This necklace reminds me of former first lady Barbara Bush. The two strands of faux pearls gleam in the light. Rhinestones are glued in on the ¾" clasp. Necklace is 7½". Signed "SARAH COV." 1950s. $75.00 – 105.00.

Round, marquee baguettes, and more round rhinestones comprise this very heavy brooch. 2¼" in diameter. 1940s to the 1950s. $120.00 – 160.00.

(Left) This pin has shallow cups with rhinestones glued in them. Rhinestones in silver roping create a star. The center has two silver ropes around the single stone. 2½". Unmarked. Late 1940s to the 1950s. $70.00 – 100.00. (Right) Silver tone over white metal. The glued-in round stones are in a "V" shape. Low quality; primitive. 1½". 1940s. Unmarked. $30.00 – 40.00.

Necklace and matching screw-back earrings. Two strands of chaton-cut rhinestones fade to the baguettes, then to the center which is made of two pear shapes around a central baguette at the top and bottom. A lone marquee in the middle with three square stones between the flexible fringe. 9". Unmarked. 1940s to the early 1950s. For the set: $140.00 – 190.00.

A single row of rhinestones flow to the drop of two rows with a fringe of baguettes and three more rows of chaton-cut rhinestones. 10⅛". Unsigned. Early 1950s to mid-1960s. $140.00 – 190.00.

This smashing brooch is very weighty with its large, pear-shaped stones that have a small rhinestone between each. Three dimensional. 1¾" diameter. 1¼" depth. Should have been signed. 1940s to the 1950s. $115.00 – 155.00.

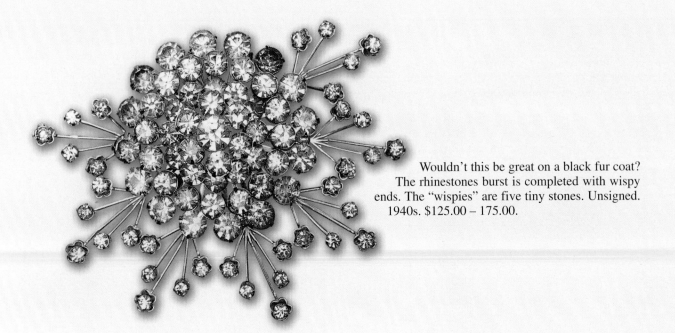

Wouldn't this be great on a black fur coat? The rhinestones burst is completed with wispy ends. The "wispies" are five tiny stones. Unsigned. 1940s. $125.00 – 175.00.

This 7¾" necklace has four sizes of round rhinestones with four silver bar swirls of pavè stones. Three sets of marquees and rounds stones on each side of the center. Fish-hook clasp. Unsigned. 1940s. $115.00 – 145.00.

Necklace and clip earrings. A single strand cascades into two with three larger rhinestones at the end of the two strands. Four stones hold the drop of four stones and a tassel of rhinestones and pearls. Unsigned. 10½". 1940s. For the set: $130.00 – 170.00.

Rhodium-plated necklace with a single strand of rhinestones. Three rhinestones on each side of the strand. Two large stones are on top of the three strand, flexible drop. 8¾". Signed "JEWELRY Fashions" on clasp. 1950s. $110.00 – 140.00.

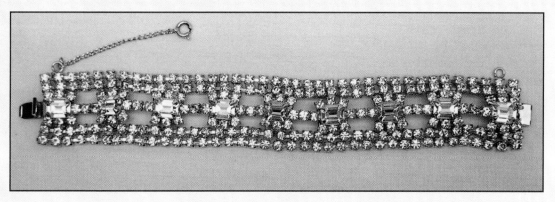

Rhodium-plated bracelet. The clasp has a safety chain. Two strands of rhinestones with a center of nine emerald stones with three small chaton-cut rhinestones between. 7⅛". Looks like Kramer or Weiss. Mid-1940s to the early 1950s. $105.00 – 145.00.

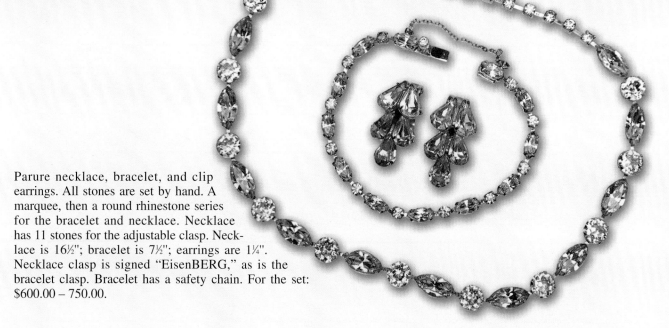

Parure necklace, bracelet, and clip earrings. All stones are set by hand. A marquee, then a round rhinestone series for the bracelet and necklace. Necklace has 11 stones for the adjustable clasp. Necklace is 16½"; bracelet is 7½"; earrings are 1¼". Necklace clasp is signed "EisenBERG," as is the bracelet clasp. Bracelet has a safety chain. For the set: $600.00 – 750.00.

Green marquees hug the small aurora borealis stones in a gold-tone leaf. Topped by five small green stones, and the center is an aurora borealis. What a great gold stem! 3⅛". Unsigned. Late 1940s to the mid-1950s. $90.00 – 130.00.

Pin and screw-on earrings have aquamarine-colored stones set in unique, gold-tone displays. Unsigned. 1950s. For the set: $70.00 – 100.00.

Fantastic fly! This brooch has pavè rhinestones in shades of green and blue over gold tone and emerald enameling. Very heavy. 2½". 1970s. Unsigned. $100.00 – 140.00.

(Left) This is a very dainty necklace which is also very lightweight. The rhinestones are handset. 1950s. Unsigned. $45.00 – 95.00. (Right) Two faux pearls separated by dainty rhinestone rings. Fish-hook clasp. 1950s. Unsigned. $45.00 – 95.00.

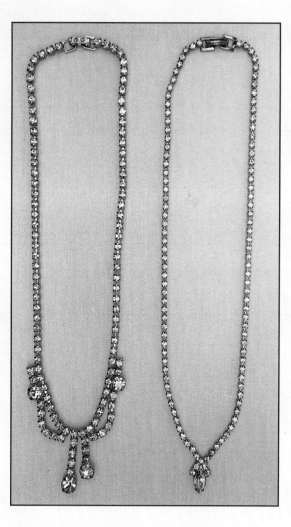

(Left) A single strand of rhinestones with fringe of two small stones and one larger one on each side dropping to a single strand of flexible dangles. 1950s. 8¼". Unsigned. $90.00 – 180.00. (Right) Silver-tone plated necklace is a single strand of rhinestones. Completed by a marquee-cut stone held by two smaller rhinestones. 7¾". 1950s. Unsigned. $85.00 – 120.00.

Demi-parure star pin and clip earrings. Round and marquee stones are glued in shallow cups. Backs are open and foiled. Five marquees in the center with five on each star. A tip on the pin. A single marquee for the center attraction of the earring. Done in silver tone. 1960s. Signed "Sarah Cov" on the pin and both clip earrings. $110.00 – 140.00.

Brooch signed "Trifari" from the 1960s. Light aqua marquees, and dark royal blue chaton rhinestones are glued in shallow cups. 2¼". 3-D in the shape of a half moon. A really bright piece. $100.00 – 130.00.

Demi-parure of clip earrings and pin done in silver tone. The pin measures 2¼" with the earrings measuring 1¾". The five tapered baguettes are handset on each of the clip earrings. Six tapered baguettes are hand set in prongs with seven aqua rhinestones hugged with pavè aurora borealis stones. All of the baguettes are open backed. Mid-to 1950s. Unmarked. $130.00 – 160.00.

(Left) Signed "Lisner." Clip earrings measure 1". Mid- to late 1950s. Dress these up or down with the wardrobe! Two dark blue emerald stones with five aurora borealis rhinestones separated by three leaves and stem. $85.00 – 115.00. (Right) Clip earrings measure 1½". Hand-set in prongs are the appealing blue tri colors. Blue marquees with a floral of baguettes and a faux pearl center. Each of the earrings is signed "MADE IN AUSTRIA." Early 1950s. $75.00 – 105.00.

Ring signed "Sterling" from the mid-1950s to the early 1960s. Six small chaton rhinestones hug the right of the ocean aqua oval stone. Stone is nicely faceted in a four prong setting. The back is open. $130.00 – 160.00.

Signed "Coro" on the center base. This is truly great for May babies! A leaf and vine design make up this necklace. Emerald marquee and round peridot rhinestones are set in the shallow cups. Adjustable chain with a fish-hook clasp. The center measures 4¾". Late 1950s to the early 1960s. $110.00 – 130.00.

Signed "Sarah Cov Pat Pend." Clip earrings measure 1¼". Round, open backed emerald stones embraced by silver leaves each holding a rhinestone. An overlay of two leaves covering the stone. Late 1950s to the early 1960s. $85.00 – 125.00.

This magnificent butterfly brooch measures 3¼" long. Unmarked. Gold-plated wings with round peridots that are prong set by hand. The pear-shaped tail is open backed and nicely cut. Mid- to late 1950s. $125.00 – 155.00.

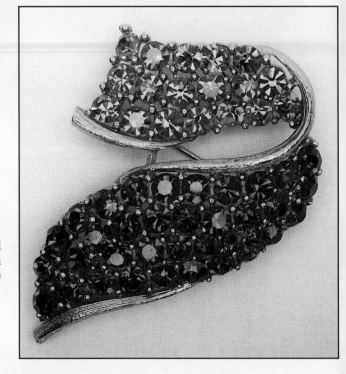

Unsigned whimsical pin from the 1950s. Done in the antique gold tone. Three rows of blue chatons on the top of the pin. The bottom row holds four rows of emerald chaton stones. The stones measure 1¾". $105.00 – 125.00.

This pin is unsigned. It measures 2⅛". Rays of blues and greens are really radiant. Done in a 3-D design. Silver tone with hand set stones. This pin is nicely weighted. 1940s – 1950s. $100.00 – 120.00.

Pin signed "MADE IN AUSTRIA." Design is 3-D. Early 1950s. Dark and light colors contrast in the emeralds and peridots. Small silver-tone flowers are raised around the peridots and deep emerald marquees. A quality piece that is weighted. $105.00 – 125.00.

(Top) Scatter pins unsigned from the early 1950s. Each measures ¾". This square shape has filigree around the center emerald. The emerald is prong set by hand. This is such a quality piece it looks like an imposter of 14K with a real emerald! $80.00 – 120.00. (Bottom) Scatter pins signed "BARCLAY." Just like Rob! 1⅛" of antiqued gold with emeralds, amethysts, and sapphire marquees separated by round amethysts with sapphire cabochon center prong set. Early 1950s. $90.00 – 130.00.

This demi-parure is signed "Lisner" on the fish-hook clasp of the necklace and each of the clip earrings. Mid- to late 1950s. Molded plastic leaves with two gold tone leaves separated by two small aurora borealis stones on each side of the link. Necklace measures 11¼" with an adjustable chain. Earrings measure ¾". $125.00 – 155.00.

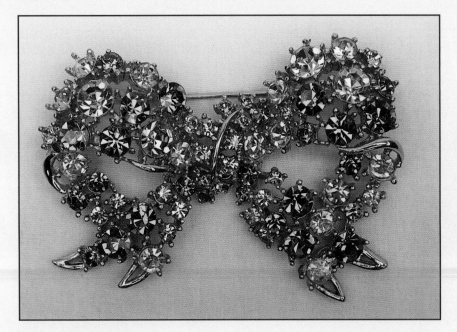

This unsigned brooch measures 2½". A bow done in 3-D guarantees to turn heads. The topaz and aqua chaton stones are set in shallow cups. Late 1940s to the mid-1950s. $115.00 – 145.00.

This defined brooch and clip earrings set are prong-set stones by hand. Earthy brown tones are used in the round and pear-shaped quality stones to make up the circle swirl design. Earrings measure 1⅛" and the brooch measures 2¼". Unmarked. 1940s to the early 1950s. $130.00 – 170.00.

Looking like autumn to me! This 2½" antiqued gold pin is twisted rope in the shape of a leaf. Five leaves hold the fall colors of peridots and citrine stones in a scattered design. Signed "AVON." Has the look of a Florenza piece. 1970s – 1980s. $60.00 – 90.00.

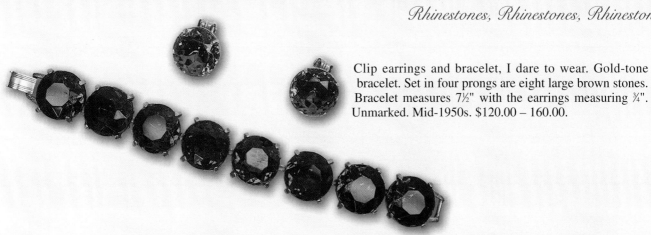

Clip earrings and bracelet, I dare to wear. Gold-tone bracelet. Set in four prongs are eight large brown stones. Bracelet measures 7½" with the earrings measuring ¾". Unmarked. Mid-1950s. $120.00 – 160.00.

I love the earthy tones of this signed Florenza necklace. Late 1950s. Seven stones in browns and greens are prong set in the center of the two peridots, three topaz stones with a drop of a small faux pearl. Adjustable chain with a fish-hook clasp. The necklace measures 10¾". $120.00 – 160.00.

Fancy free brooch signed "Trifari." Done in a gold tone with marquees and round stones. Two tones of topaz colors are used. The stones are set in shallow cups. Three marquees and three round stones are raised to create a 3-D look. This 2¼" pin is weighted. Early to late 1950s. $100.00 – 130.00.

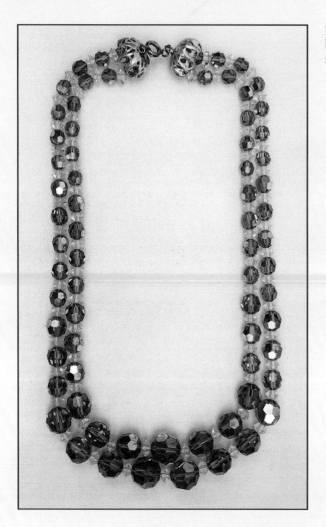

8⅜" necklace of aurora borealis in two strands. Crystal and brown beads are hand strung on string. The beads have some give on the strand. Weighted. Early 1940s. Unmarked. $105.00 – 135.00.

A charming flower brooch in a two-tone pink. Three small peridot rhinestones make up the stem. Stones are glued in shallow cups. Measures 2¾". Unmarked. Early 1950s. $75.00 – 105.00.

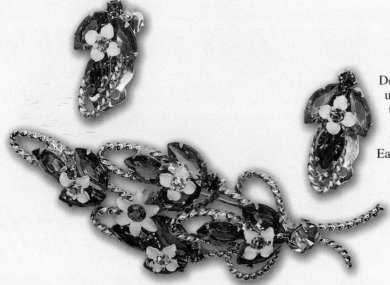

Delicate pin and clip earrings in gold tone are unsigned. The marquees are open backed on the tree of flowers. Prong-set marquees with small chaton rhinestones glued in the enameled flowers. Pin measures 3", earrings measure ¾". Early 1950s. $90.00 – 110.00.

This smart necklace converts to a small hand mirror. Done in gold tone with pink stones glued around the hand-painted floral scene. I question that this chain is the original. Mirror measures 3½". Unsigned. Mid-1950s to early 1960s. Clever piece! $100.00 – 130.00.

* A sparkling design for a sparkling brooch! Measures 3½" and is unsigned. Marquees are raised and weighted. Chaton-cut rhinestones and marquees are prong set. Early 1950s. $110.00 – 130.00.

An exquisite aurora borealis rhinestone pin from the 1940s! Prong-set aurora borealis rhinestones make up the base with the aurora beads set up off of the base. Two rows of aurora borealis rhinestones with a large aurora borealis stone in the center to create a floral design. Measures 1½" and is unmarked. $85.00 – 115.00.

Trifari in the original box. Set of signed pieces. This necklace is signed on the clasp, and the earrings are each signed on the clip, "PAT PEND TRIFARI." Silver-tone rope chain with a fabulously designed center. Stones scream quality! Necklace measures 7⅛" with the center 2½" in width. Earrings measure 1¼". Early 1960s. $185.00 – 245.00.

This silver-tone brooch is a delicate spray of rhinestones in marquee and round shapes. All prong set. Measures 3". Unmarked. Mid-1940s to early 1950s. $105.00 – 135.00.

Superb square designed brooch in a 3-D effect. Chaton and emerald shapes complete the square. A center emerald stone. The placement of the pin on the back tells me it is to be worn in the shape of a diamond. Done in silver tone which makes the pin look heavy, and it is. 1940s. Measures 1¾" and is unsigned. $100.00 – 140.00.

Simple, yet elegant brooch signed "Eisenberg." Done in silver tone measuring 1¾". From the 1940s. Prong-set emerald stones with a raised arrow of pavè rhinestones over each side. One stone on the arrow is missing. $110.00 – 150.00.

A wonderful brooch in silver tone measuring 2½" from the late 1940s, unsigned. The stones are prong set by hand with the marquees measuring ½". The chaton-cut rhinestones are true all-around quality. $105.00 – 135.00.

Clip earrings signed "WEISS" are weighted! Silver tone. Quality pear-shaped and chaton rhinestones are hand set in prongs with a center round stone. Late 1940s to the early 1950s. $90.00 – 130.00.

2¾" open airy pin from the early 1950s. Unmarked. Seven black glass marquees set by hand with a small round black glass. Gold filigree overlays set on four of the stones. A gold leaf and filigree stem on this beauty. $85.00 – 115.00.

Signed Sarah Coventry brooch measures 2¼". From the late 1950s to the early 1960s. Plating is done in a gold tone. Stones are glued in shallow cups. Eight rows of rhinestones in a swirl design with eight raised gold-tone swirls to embrace the center of the rhinestones. $85.00 – 115.00.

(Left) 1½" pin signed "NOSN," from the late 1950s. Gold tone with multicolored dainty stones that are prong set on four gold-tone leafs. Weighted. $55.00 – 85.00. (Center) 2⅛" butterfly pin, unsigned. Gold-tone over metal with glued-in aurora borealis stones for the wings. Four faux pearls for the body and two rubies for the eyes. Late 1950s. $55.00 – 95.00. (Right) Owl pin from the late 1950s measures 1¾" long. Red chaton rhinestones are glued in shallow cups. Done in gold tone. Unmarked. $55.00 – 95.00.

(Left) Heart pin. Great for Valentine's Day! Gold tone with multicolored rhinestones that are prong set. The center has a faux pearl. This measures 1⅛". Unsigned. From the 1960s. $45.00 – 65.00. (Right) Rose pin, 2" long, from the 1970s to the early 1980s. Signed "AVON." Gold tone with a single pink pear-shaped stone on the side of a leaf. Three leaves hug the stem with the rose to top it off. $40.00 – 60.00.

Heavy brooch, signed "Coro," measures 2½". Flashing to the eye are aurora borealis and molded plastic in rainbow colors. A silver-tone stem holds a set of small leaves at the top and bottom. Open backed. 1950s. $85.00 – 115.00.

Brooch and clip earrings, unsigned. The salmon-colored marquees with open back are prong set by hand. Nicely faceted stones. Six small aurora borealis stones are scattered throughout the brooch. Brooch measures 2½" with the earrings measuring 1¼". Late 1940s. $135.00 – 175.00.

Unsigned 2" pin. All stones are open in the back. Amethyst oval, round, and pear-shaped glass of nice sizes make up this delight. The center bursts with six small bars topped with small rhinestones. Four small rhinestones are missing. Gold tone over metal. 1940s. $115.00 – 135.00.

Sizzling 2¾" brooch from the 1940s. Silver tone with stones prong set by hand. Two rows of chaton rhinestones around the six light amethyst marquees. Two small and two large round rhinestones scattered. The light amethyst stones are open backed. Unmarked. $115.00 – 135.00.

This brooch is done in a gold wash over metal. Prong set amethyst stones are open backed. Eight amethyst ovals surround the center gold flower with the rhinestones glued in shallow cups. Heavy design of three filigree flowers in a gold tone circle with one small stem from the vine. Measures 2¾" and is unsigned. Late 1930s to mid-1940s. $120.00 – 160.00.

May Day. Remember when you would wrap the pole in the high school gym for the May Day festivities? This pin measures 1½" and is unsigned. Stones are prong set by hand. Emerald marquees with gold-tone half moons swirled over the marquee. Six small round emerald stones separate the half moon. All stones are open backed. Mid-1940s to the early 1950s. $110.00 – 150.00.

This fun pin is from the 1940s. It is gold backed and measures 1½". Unmarked. The beads are hand painted in reds and golds. Four are done in aurora borealis. The center holds a cranberry colored, oddly shaped plastic, with a center rhinestone. Each bead is tipped with a small prong set rhinestone. $80.00 – 110.00.

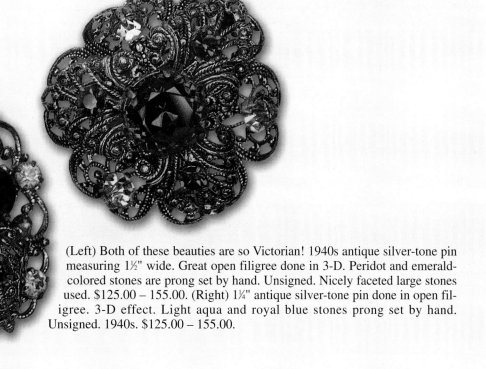

(Left) Both of these beauties are so Victorian! 1940s antique silver-tone pin measuring 1½" wide. Great open filigree done in 3-D. Peridot and emerald-colored stones are prong set by hand. Unsigned. Nicely faceted large stones used. $125.00 – 155.00. (Right) 1¼" antique silver-tone pin done in open filigree. 3-D effect. Light aqua and royal blue stones prong set by hand. Unsigned. 1940s. $125.00 – 155.00.

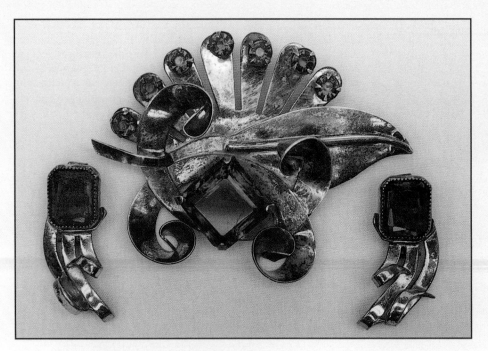

Brooch is signed "BROOKCRAFT STERLING." Both earrings are signed "STERLING." 1940s. Gold wash over sterling. Stones are prong set by hand. Great design of swirls off of the fanned leaf. Emerald stones are open backed. Stones in earrings are bezel set. Brooch measures 2½" and the earrings are 1⅛". $160.00 – 200.00.

Appealing 1940s pin, unsigned. Stones are prong set by hand. Three pear-shaped dark topaz stones with two sizes of round rhinestones. This picture is deceiving; the pin only measures 1½". $95.00 – 135.00.

Brilliant designed pin measures 1¾", from the 1940s. The three-fold citrine colors are prong set by hand. Pin done in 3-D. Design of a circle in a square with citrine chaton stones as the circle. Two marquees make the square and four topaz chaton stones circle the brown center stone. Unsigned. $105.00 – 135.00.

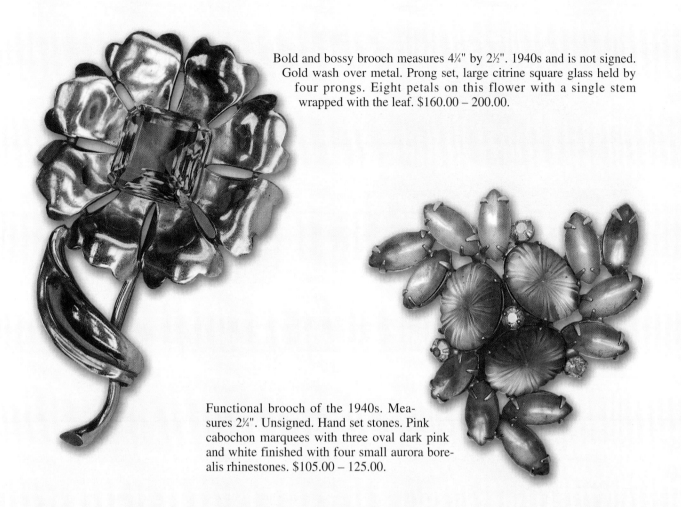

Bold and bossy brooch measures 4¼" by 2½". 1940s and is not signed. Gold wash over metal. Prong set, large citrine square glass held by four prongs. Eight petals on this flower with a single stem wrapped with the leaf. $160.00 – 200.00.

Functional brooch of the 1940s. Measures 2¼". Unsigned. Hand set stones. Pink cabochon marquees with three oval dark pink and white finished with four small aurora borealis rhinestones. $105.00 – 125.00.

Splendid flowing design makes up this unsigned brooch. Measures 2¾" and is from the 1940s. Stones are hand set. Arranged in small and large sizes of light and dark blue marquees with small aurora borealis. Closed backing done in silver tone. $100.00 – 130.00.

To wear this brooch you must be flashy. Done in 3-D effect with aurora borealis stones, and is heavy. Measures 2¼". 1940s. $115.00 – 135.00.

Attractive brooch is signed "Austria." Astounding workmanship in this piece. Five flowers of teardrops with dark aqua round stones embrace the center flower consisting of dark aqua round stones. Stones are hand set and done in silver tone. Measures 2⅛", 1950s. $105.00 – 145.00.

(Outer) 16¼" necklace. Unsigned. Silver-tone plating from the 1950s. Two sizes of prong-set, chaton stones are used and the larger row is fringing. One set of two small stones complete each side. A finished fish-hook clasp is utilized. $115.00 – 135.00. (Inner) 1½" silver-tone clip earrings from the 1950s. Excellent quality, large stones used for this unmarked beauty. Weighted. $90.00 – 120.00.

(Left) Clip earrings measure 2½". One clip is signed "GALE." 1950s. Four rows of chaton-cut rhinestones all prong set by hand. Flexible rows. $90.00 – 130.00. (Right) 1¼" clip earrings. All stones prong set by hand. Five emerald stones separated with two small rhinestones and one large center stone. 1950s. Unsigned. $80.00 – 120.00.

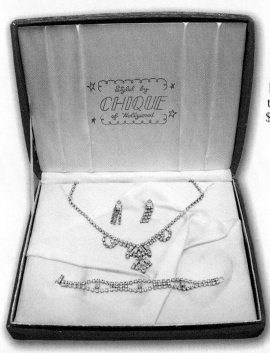

Parure in the original CHIQUE red velvet box. This red velvet box is styled by CHIQUE of Hollywood. Never out of the box, this set boasts of clip earrings, necklace, and bracelet. Necklace has small fringe with a center drop. The drop is stiff to move, and has seven baguette stones with chaton stones. 1950s. I did not pull these out of the box to measure or to see if they are signed. $200.00 – 275.00.

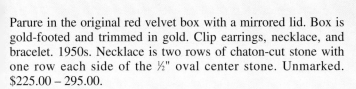

Parure in the original red velvet box with a mirrored lid. Box is gold-footed and trimmed in gold. Clip earrings, necklace, and bracelet. 1950s. Necklace is two rows of chaton-cut stone with one row each side of the ½" oval center stone. Unmarked. $225.00 – 295.00.

Stunning demi-parure pin and clip earrings set. Three light amethyst rhinestones are surrounded by small, dark amethysts in a circle. Five marquee-cut, aurora borealis stones are set outside the circle. A fringe of five stones, with a large center stone, completes the work. Late 1940s. Signed "Austria" on the pin and each of the clip earrings. For the set: $135.00 – 185.00.

Detail and quality. Cute as can be Siamese kitty cat! Reminds me of our beloved Muffy. All stones are set by hand. Chaton-cut rhinestones outline the corpse of the cat. Black-colored pear, marquee, and round rhinestones are used for the eyes, ears, and mouth. Silver filigree for the whiskers. Silver rods for the nose structure and tail. Cat measures 4⅛" and its chain is 9⅛". Unsigned, unreal! Late 1940s to the 1950s. $150.00 – 190.00.

Demi-parure clip earrings and bracelet. All stones are set by hand. Two emeralds in light yellow with topaz marquees in an every-other stone pattern. Bracelet has a safety chain. Quality! Great for a November person. Bracelet is 5¾" and the earrings are 1½". Each of the earrings and the bracelet are signed "Coro USA Pat Pending." 1940s to the 1950s. $125.00 – 165.00.

(Left) These clip earrings have four marquees topped off with a round stone. Unsigned. 1¼". 1950s. $55.00 – 85.00. (Center) These clips have two thick gold ropes with dark colored aurora borealis beads in the center. Unsigned. 1950s. $40.00 – 60.00. (Right) One topaz stone is glued in the center of the five gold petals. Unsigned. 1950s. Gold tone. $30.00 – 45.00.

Demi-parure cuff bracelet done in mosaic. The stones are set by hand. They come in various shades of brown in pear and emerald shapes. Round topaz and red rhinestones with three small, light yellow rhinestones. Larger stones are also employed for this set. Earrings measure 1¼." 1950s. Unsigned. $190.00 – 230.00.

Demi-parure of compact and bracelet. Emerald and ruby cabochons set in heavy white enamel with rhinestones in groups of four on bracelet and compact. Compact holds the original powder puff that reads, "Evans." I don't know if this set was ever used. Compact 2½". 1950s. Unsigned, unreal. $250.00 – 350.00.

Demi-parure brooch and clip earrings set. Round and marquee faux pearls and rhinestones with a prong-set aurora borealis center stone. Done in three dimensions. 2½." Each of the clip earrings, as well as the brooch is signed, "Judy Lee." Late 1940s to the 1950s. $170.00 – 230.00.

Silver-tone plated brooch with aurora borealis rhinestones glued in the centers of these flowers. The flowers have five petals. 3¼". 1950s. Unsigned. $90.00 – 140.00.

This gold-tone necklace has rhinestone glued in shallow cups with eight gold plastic bars. Three stones are missing. 4½" adjustable chain with a fish-hook clasp. Unsigned. 1950s. $55.00 – 75.00.

(Top) Pastel-colored stones glued in shallow cups with emerald flowers and leaves in nice detail. A topaz-colored, oval center finishes the piece. Stone is nicely fastened. Filigree is used in the center. 2¼". 1930s. $80.00 – 120.00. (Bottom) This white metal pin has pastel stones glued in deeper cups, which form the shape of a flower. Eight stones surround the flower. 2". Unsigned. 1930s. $60.00 – 100.00.

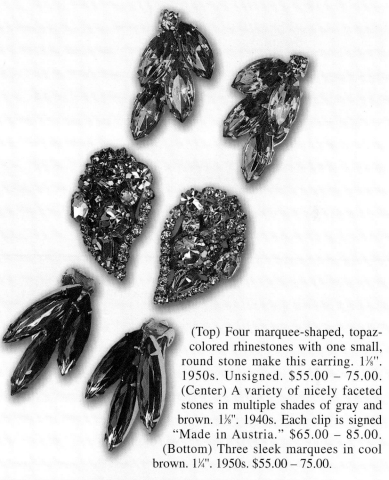

(Top) Four marquee-shaped, topaz-colored rhinestones with one small, round stone make this earring. 1⅛". 1950s. Unsigned. $55.00 – 75.00. (Center) A variety of nicely faceted stones in multiple shades of gray and brown. 1⅛". 1940s. Each clip is signed "Made in Austria." $65.00 – 85.00. (Bottom) Three sleek marquees in cool brown. 1¼". 1950s. $55.00 – 75.00.

Demi-parure pin and clip earrings set. Two rows of aurora borealis and two rows of dark pink rhinestones are varied every other row. 2¼" pin; 1⅛" earrings. 1950s. Unsigned. For the set: $130.00 – 180.00.

Pendant missing the original chain. White metal with a silver tone brushed over. Filigree in open design flows to the large center of dark blue glass. The glass is open backed. Measures 3⅛". The stone is 1¼". This antique beauty is from the late 1900s to the 1930s. $200.00 – 300.00.

Pendant converts to a brooch. The magnificent FLORENZA from the mid-1920s to the early 1930s measures 2¼" with the purple glass measuring 1⅛". The center stone is foiled on the back. Aurora borealis and amethysts are set around the center stone on the silver edges. $180.00 – 280.00.

This elegant brooch is unmarked. Open filigree work separated by solid gold-tone bars. The bezel emerald stone is open backed. Gold tone brushed over metal. Measures 2¼". The stone is 1¼". Mid-1920s to the early 1930s. $170.00 – 270.00.

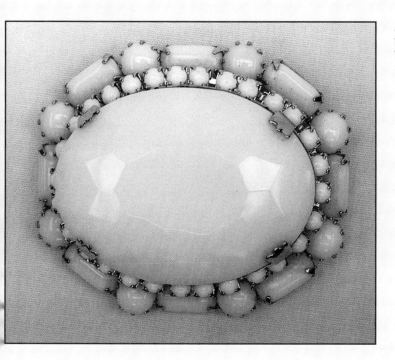

A sleek brooch, with the oval center in white milk glass that is open backed. Round and emerald cabochons all set by hand. Gold tone. Measures 2" and is unsigned. Early 1930s to mid-1940s. $170.00 – 230.00.

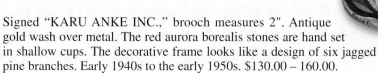

Signed "KARU ANKE INC.," brooch measures 2". Antique gold wash over metal. The red aurora borealis stones are hand set in shallow cups. The decorative frame looks like a design of six jagged pine branches. Early 1940s to the early 1950s. $130.00 – 160.00.

Primitive, yet appealing brooch from the 1940s is weighted. Nice sized, well cut purple stones, two large and three medium, are glued in the sets. Rhinestones are sprinkled about. Unmarked and measures 2". Gold tone. $120.00 – 160.00.

This vivid silver-tone bar pin of the 1940s measures 3¼" wide. Heavy. Deep pink cabochons in a flower design with a silver ball between each of the three flowers. Unsigned. $95.00 – 135.00.

KRAMER STERLING brooch is mystical in design. Round and oval rhinestones set around a raised center of nine chaton rhinestones with the oval center. Three silver wires flow off the side of the center, each tipped with a rhinestone. All prong-set stones by hand. 1940 to the early 1950s. Measures 3". $140.00 – 180.00.

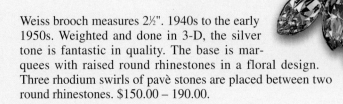

Weiss brooch measures 2½". 1940s to the early 1950s. Weighted and done in 3-D, the silver tone is fantastic in quality. The base is marquees with raised round rhinestones in a floral design. Three rhodium swirls of pavè stones are placed between two round rhinestones. $150.00 – 190.00.

Screw-back earrings are each signed "STERLING." The pin is unsigned and measures 1¾". Prong-set rhinestones with open back foiled marquees for the border with round stones circling the center oval stone. 1940s. $110.00 – 160.00.

SARAH COVENTRY pin from the 1950s measures 2½". This is a light, simple design of five aqua marquees that are glued in the shallow cups. Each is set between a silver leaf-like enclosure. Baguettes are down the center spine with small rhinestones around the leaves. $85.00 – 115.00.

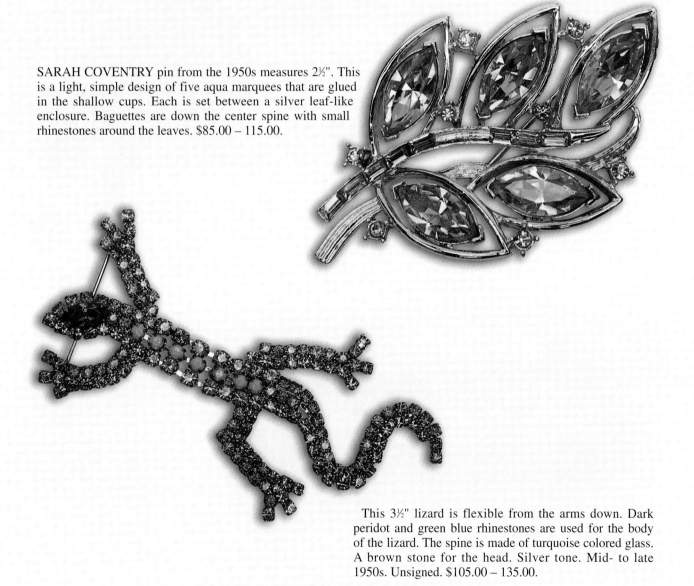

This 3½" lizard is flexible from the arms down. Dark peridot and green blue rhinestones are used for the body of the lizard. The spine is made of turquoise colored glass. A brown stone for the head. Silver tone. Mid- to late 1950s. Unsigned. $105.00 – 135.00.

This 1950s car pin is definitely uptown. The chaton-cut rhinestones are in the shape of a car with black stones used as the tires, window, wheel, and light. All stones are set by hand, and the pin is done in silver tone. Measures 2¼" and is unmarked. $105.00 – 135.00.

Sophistication speaks with this rhodium brooch. I can't believe this is unmarked. Heavy pavè rhinestones make the 3-D flower. Measures 2¾". From the late 1940s. $125.00 – 175.00.

This 1950s cab reminds me of the old cabs in Pittsburgh. Topaz, black, and crystal rhinestones make up this car. Silver tone. Stones set by hand. Measures 2¾". Unmarked. $110.00 – 140.00.

This sparkling bow should be worn for the holidays. Measures 2½" and is unsigned. Chaton rhinestones make up the flexible ribbon. Baguettes are in the center of the ribbon. Quality stones. Late 1940s to the early 1950s. $125.00 – 175.00.

This bold brooch is signed "KRAMER OF NEW YORK." Baguettes and round rhinestones set in an every-other pattern for the base with two rows of clustered rhinestones surrounding the emerald square center. All prong set by hand. Measures 1¾". 1950s. $85.00 – 135.00.

Signed "MADE IN AUSTRIA" brooch from the early 1950s. Wispy in design. Rhinestones are prong set by hand. Delicate. Measures 2¼". $75.00 – 125.00.

Ebony and ivory marquee cabochons border the silver swirl center with prong-set small black rhinestones with a large center black stone. Backing is detailed filigree work. Measures 1¾" and is not signed. 1950s. $85.00 – 125.00.

Butterflies are free to fly, fly away. Heavy WEISS butterfly brooch from the late 1940s to the early 1950s. Four sections of white glass for wings and a body of large and small marquee cabochons. Small red stones for the accents. One stone is missing on the top right. 2¼" wide. $90.00 – 130.00.

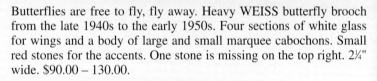

(Center) Antique gold-tone clock signed "1928 JAPAN MOVEMENT BASE METAL BEZEL STAINLESS STEEL BACK." 1980s. $40.00 – 70.00. (Outer) Unmarked necklace. Classic looking, dates 1950s. Measures 7¾". Clasp is a floral design. Chain is made of gold-tone links. The center is a drop of oval cabochons and small pink rhinestones. The drop is moveable. All stones are glued in. $120.00 – 160.00.

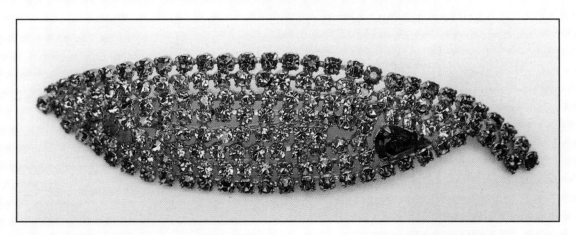

MADE IN AUSTRIA brooch measures 3¾". Elaborate style offers small chaton pink rhinestones with a single pear-shaped stone at the bottom right of the pin. Early 1950s. $120.00 – 170.00.

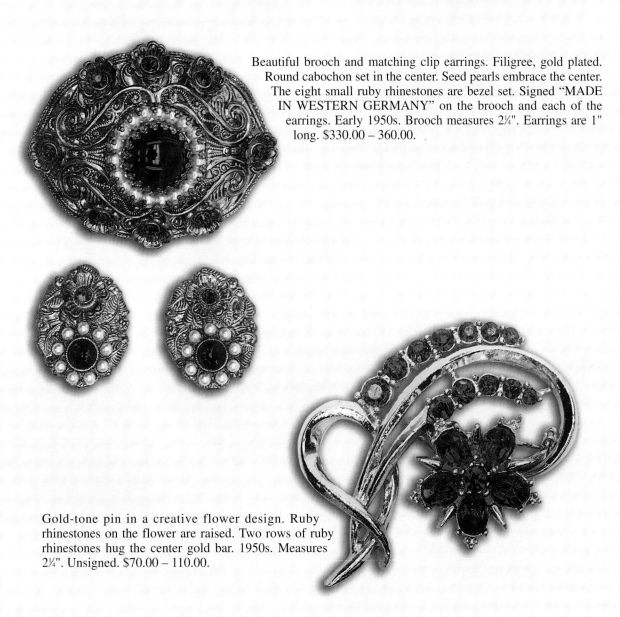

Beautiful brooch and matching clip earrings. Filigree, gold plated. Round cabochon set in the center. Seed pearls embrace the center. The eight small ruby rhinestones are bezel set. Signed "MADE IN WESTERN GERMANY" on the brooch and each of the earrings. Early 1950s. Brooch measures 2¼". Earrings are 1" long. $330.00 – 360.00.

Gold-tone pin in a creative flower design. Ruby rhinestones on the flower are raised. Two rows of ruby rhinestones hug the center gold bar. 1950s. Measures 2¼". Unsigned. $70.00 – 110.00.

Clip earrings signed WEISS measure 1½". Aurora borealis stones encompass the two royal blue marquees. A pear-shaped dark blue stone and a round stone in light aqua set off to the side. Gold tone. Stones are hand set. 1950s. $80.00 – 120.00.

Uptown set from the 1950s. The pin measures 2¼"; screw-on earrings ¾". Six topaz marquees tip off the seven chaton rhinestones in a circle design. The center is a circle with a larger center stone. $90.00 – 120.00.

Necklace and pierced earrings from the 1950s. The necklace measures 8¾" with the earrings measuring 1¼" long. Silver tone. Stones are set by hand. Chaton rhinestones with seven royal blue emeralds topping off the five sets of flexible fringe. A fish-hook clasp closes to the single royal blue rhinestone. Unsigned. $140.00 – 180.00.

This 1950s hand set brooch is sleek in the best way. Topaz marquees then aurora borealis stones embrace the four large round topaz stones. 3-D effect. $115.00 – 135.00.

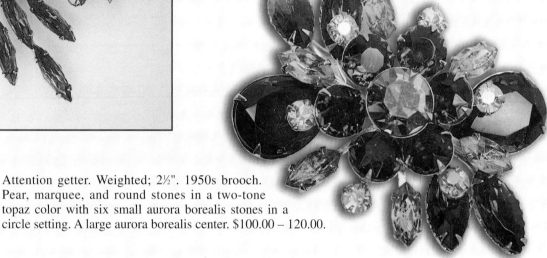

Attention getter. Weighted; 2½". 1950s brooch. Pear, marquee, and round stones in a two-tone topaz color with six small aurora borealis stones in a circle setting. A large aurora borealis center. $100.00 – 120.00.

A variety of colors of stones make this vivid. 2½" brooch with clip earrings. Stones are set on tips of gold bars in a series of two. Center is a flower with small light citrine stones on every other flower separated by a larger stone. All stones are hand set. Unsigned. $110.00 – 140.00.

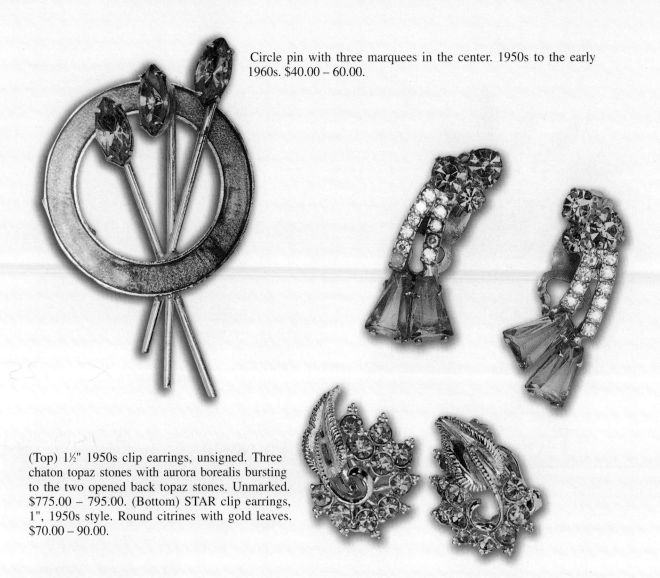

Circle pin with three marquees in the center. 1950s to the early 1960s. $40.00 – 60.00.

(Top) 1½" 1950s clip earrings, unsigned. Three chaton topaz stones with aurora borealis bursting to the two opened back topaz stones. Unmarked. $775.00 – 795.00. (Bottom) STAR clip earrings, 1", 1950s style. Round citrines with gold leaves. $70.00 – 90.00.

(Left) 1" brown plastic bead clip earrings marked "Western Germany." Early 1950s. $55.00 – 85.00. (Center) Clip earrings. Unmarked. 1". 1950s. Center of chaton topaz stones with border of delicate gold leaves. $45.00 – 55.00. (Right) Unmarked pair. Two sizes of marquees with a center aurora borealis stone. All hand set. 1¼". 1950s. $65.00 – 85.00.

Unmarked 2¼" cross in antique gold. Four oval amethysts and round center with faux turquoise stones on the sides of the stones. 1970s. $90.00 – 130.00.

All unmarked in this set. Necklace measures 9⅛" with a ½" clasp, clip earrings 1¼", and bracelet is 7¾". 1940s. If you were born in February, this set is a perfect fit for you. $155.00 – 185.00.

Saucy silver-tone plated brooch with larger sized pear and round cabochons set around the pink chaton cut rhinestones with a round center. Mid-1940s to the late 1950s. 2¼". $115.00 – 135.00.

Two bedazzling shades of amethysts are chaton cut for this typically whimsical 1940s flower. Unsigned. $85.00 – 105.00.

Nicely faceted pink glass beads which are strung tightly on a double heavy string. 7⅛". 1920s to the early 1930s. Stamped "1/20 12K GF." $120.00 – 150.00.

If your birthday were in July, this would be the perfect piece for you. Bezel-set, round red cabochon center with four small cabochons on each side. Resembles a compass rose. 2" in diameter. 1950s. $80.00 – 120.00.

(Left) This 1½" 1940s, gold plated over metal ribbon shares a center splash of rhinestones set in shallow cups. Unsigned. $80.00 – 120.00. (Right) This fantastic flower is 1¾" in diameter with five petals. 1940s. $90.00 – 130.00.

A stunning silver bracelet which is quite weighty with dome-shaped, blue, cut glass. Two large rhinestones are between each, and the bracelet has a safety chain. Unsigned. 6". $125.00 – 155.00.

1950s. Chain, 11¾" and the pendant is 2½". This is one classy cross with four pearls used as rhinestones' appendage separators. $90.00 – 120.00.

Each of the earrings in this pair measures ¾" in diameter. Late 1940s to the early 1950s. Looks like Germany. $55.00 – 75.00. (Pin) 1⅛" in diameter; a super star! 1940s to the early 1950s. $55.00 – 75.00.

(Earrings) ¾" clips. Pear-shaped and from the 1940s. $50.00 – 80.00. (Pin) A dazzling array of marquee-cut stones in a myriad of colors. $120.00 – 160.00.

(Top) Unsigned pin and clip earrings set from the 1950s. Measures 1¾" long. For the earrings: $50.00 – 90.00. For the pin: $95.00 – 125.00. (Bottom) This charming ID bracelet measures 7" and has a raised flower with eight chaton-cut rhinestones. $90.00 – 120.00.

(Center) 1⅛" ribbon pin with multicolored stones. A single blue center. 1940s. $ 50.00 – 70.00. (Outer) Seven gold-tone links with a single chaton stone separated by six flowers in light blue topaz with a center rhinestone. 9" adjustable staple chain with a fish-hook clasp and ball. Necklace measures 8¼". Signed "Lisner." 1950s. $120.00 – 150.00.

(Top) 2½" pin from the 1930s in white metal. Three rows of chaton rhinestones glued in the shallow cups. Unmarked. $95.00 – 125.00. (Bottom) 2¾" 1930s white metal pin. Center row of larger stones with smaller border stones. In a half-moon shape. Unmarked. $75.00 – 105.00.

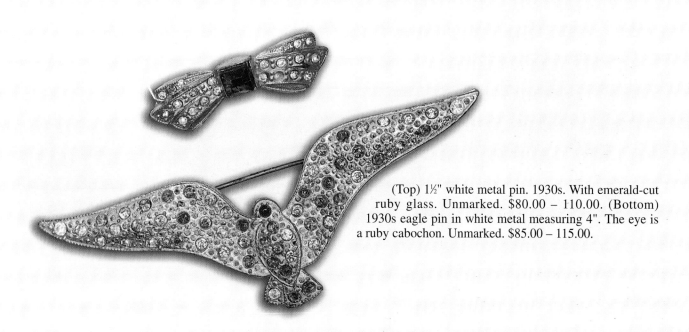

(Top) 1½" white metal pin. 1930s. With emerald-cut ruby glass. Unmarked. $80.00 – 110.00. (Bottom) 1930s eagle pin in white metal measuring 4". The eye is a ruby cabochon. Unmarked. $85.00 – 115.00.

1940s bold brooch in silver tone with round marquee and emerald rhinestones in 3-D. Weighted and unsigned. Measures 2¼". $125.00 – 165.00.

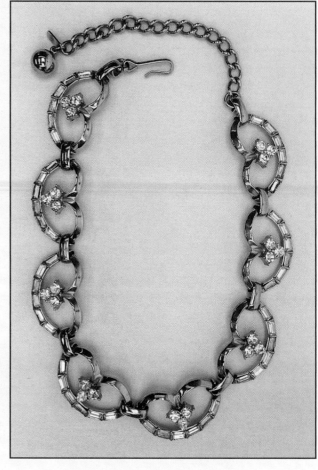

Gold-tone choker with eight hearts connected by a link. 4¼" adjustable chain with a fish-hook clasp necklace that measures 11½." 1950s. Tag reads, "TARA." $105.00 – 125.00.

Wow, an owl! Flexible topaz marquees are set in gold tone. Eyes are brown cabochons. 3¼" owl; 12" chain. Unsigned. Early 1970s. $105.00 – 125.00.

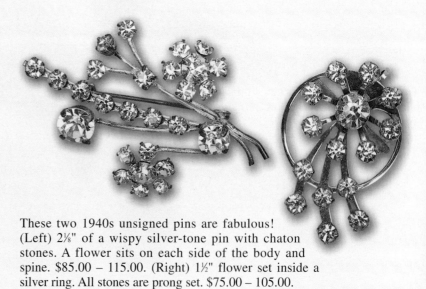

These two 1940s unsigned pins are fabulous! (Left) 2⅛" of a wispy silver-tone pin with chaton stones. A flower sits on each side of the body and spine. $85.00 – 115.00. (Right) 1½" flower set inside a silver ring. All stones are prong set. $75.00 – 105.00.

Bracelet and clip earrings. 1950s. Bracelet is 7¼." Unsigned. $120.00 – 150.00.

A flexible pink pin with a tassel suspended from the bottom. 1960s. 3½." Signed "Sara Cov." $75.00 – 105.00.

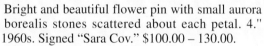

Bright and beautiful flower pin with small aurora borealis stones scattered about each petal. 4." 1960s. Signed "Sara Cov." $100.00 – 130.00.

(Left) Whimsical pin of baguettes and pavè rhinestones with a sprinkle of red stones. Eye catching. 1½". 1940s to the early 1950s. Unsigned. $50.00 – 80.00. (Right) This Wahoo fish makes me say yahoo! It has baguettes and two sizes of rhinestones on the body of the fish. Marquees comprise the tail. 1½". Signed "Bogoff." 1950s. $85.00 – 115.00.

Christmas and Holiday

(Left) Cute stocking pin. Gift boxes are crammed into the top of the boot while there are five green leaves and two faux seed pearls used for snow. Signed "Art." 1970s. 1½" long. $25.00 – 45.00. (Right) What a stocking stuffer and Christmas kitten! This gold-tone and red enameling pin has a kitten snug in a boot! The kitten's eyes are small, red rhinestones. 1960s. Unsigned. Measures 1½". $25.00 – 45.00.

(Left) This candle really burns bright! A tear-shaped red rhinestone is employed for the flame with a circle of gold for glow. White enameling makes the dripping wax; red enameling for the berries and green for the holly. Base has blue, yellow, red, and green-glued stones. Late 1960s to the mid-1970s. It is signed, but the signature is illegible. $30.00 – 50.00. (Right) Another smart Christmas brooch. Three tear-shaped crystal flames with two golden glowing circles. Green and red enameling at the base with pine and a polished bow. Snow is flitted about the pin. Unsigned. Measures 1½". Late 1960s to the mid-1970s. $25.00 – 45.00.

(Left) Who would crave a cornucopia stuffed with gifts? Emerald leaves with multiple clear rhinestones and careful detailing to the presents. Measures 2¼". Signed "B.J." Late 1960s to the mid-1970s. $30.00 – 50.00. (Right) We want our packages delivered by this on-the-way sleigh! 1960s. $30.00 – 50.00.

(Left and right) These swanky Christmas candles share many similarities. For starters, their bases are composed of gold toning. Neither candle is signed. Mid-1960s to the late 1960s. (Left) Measures 2". A crystal tear-shaped flame is glued in with white enameling for wax. An enameled sprig of holly holds berries. $25.00 – 45.00. (Right) Measures 1¾". A blue tear-shaped flame is glued in with a red enameled candle, hugged by a sprig of holly. $25.00 – 45.00.

(Left) A pretty winter green enameled, holly leaf pin. Measures 2½". Unsigned. Late 1960s. $25.00 – 45.00. (Right) Glued-in faux pearls drip from the gold tone winter leaves. There are five small rhinestones on the piece and a glued-in, winter green stone at the base. 1960s. Unsigned. 2¼" long. $30.00 – 50.00.

(Left) This heavy, Christmas basket pin has evergreen-colored enameling for the basket. Nicely detailed, rope-styled handle. 1½". Unsigned. 1960s. $30.00 – 50.00. (Right) I wish this snowflake would fall on me! Five pair of winter colored pierced earrings act as the wondrous colors of this perfect flake! 2¼". Looks like Avon. Late 1970s to the early 1980s. $20.00 – 40.00.

Christmas tree pin and pierced earrings set. Christmas gift boxes are stacked on this tree. Glued-on plastic beads and a star top the tree. Tree measures 2¾" long; earrings are 1" long. Set was in the original Avon box. Late 1970s to the early 1980s. $20.00 – 30.00.

Silver-tone hinged bracelet with excellent detail! 1960s. Cute earrings. Rhinestones are scattered on the snowy white earrings. For the set: $110.00 – 150.00.

Nice necklace and marvelous matching clip earrings. The earrings are made of a large bead suspended from a small bead. Two strands of red, plastic beads are strung on red strings to make the necklace. Finishes with a large, fish-hook clasp. Measures 6½". Early 1950s. Unsigned. $30.00 – 60.00.

(Left) Oh! Christmas tree, how lovely are your branches! Gold wash over plating with small green, blue, citrine, and red rhinestones embedded. Rhinestones are in groups of four on ten places on the tree. A citrine is used for the star. 2½". Unsigned. $50.00 – 100.00. (Right) A sturdy Christmas tree pin on gold wash plating. An amalgam of colored stones are glued into the pin, and there are etched stones for the background. 2¼" long. 1950s to the 1960s. Unsigned. $50.00 – 100.00.

(Left) Green over gold for the pin with six gold balls and a star on the top. 2". Unsigned. 1960s. $30.00 – 60.00. (Center) Sharply defined pines with small green, white, red, and blue rhinestones. One stone is missing on the bottom right. A finished pot with gold rivets. 2¼". 1950s to the 1960s. Unsigned. $40.00 – 70.00. (Right) Christmas-y rhinestones in white, red, and green. A green, pear-shaped stone tops the tree. Nice quality. 1¾". Early 1960s. $50.00 – 105.00.

(Left) Rocking wreath! Very heavy with silver-tone holly leaves and gold berries. 1½". 1960s. Unsigned. $50.00 – 100.00. (Right) Silver tone with Christmas green and red enameling. Three gold-ish pine cones and silvery red berries. Very Christmas cute! Late 1950s. 1½". Unsigned. $40.00 – 70.00.

(Left) Plastic wreath with pine green holly and red berries. A bow finishes the piece. 1¾". 1950s. Unsigned. $35.00 – 65.00. (Right) Quality green and white rhinestones with a gold bow on the top and a center red stone. 1¼". Not signed; I am in shock about this! Early 1960s. $55.00 – 100.00.

(Left) Pierced bell earrings. A gold bell with light metal ribbon in red, green, and gold that is suspended from a red, satin rope. 2¼". 1970s. Unsigned. $15.00 – 35.00. (Center) Better than your average bell pin. A red, enameled ribbon with a drop of three chains holding each bell. Rather flexible. 2¼" long. 1950s. Unsigned. $20.00 – 40.00. (Right) Silver tone with green and red enameling bell pin. A bow is used to top. Super cute! 1¼". 1960s. Unsigned. $30.00 – 50.00.

(Left) Unique and cool guitar gift pin. Has three holly leaves with berries and a ribbon. A coat charm is suspended from the side. 1950s. 3". $30.00 – 60.00. (Right) Lovely holly pin made of gold plating. Very heavy with enameling. Six red berries are raised from the leaf. Pavè rhinestones complete the top. 2". Early to mid-1960s. Unsigned. $45.00 – 85.00.

(Top left) Pierced poinsettia earrings. Unsigned, but looks like Avon. 1970s. $15.00 – 35.00. (Bottom left) Winter white poinsettia pin converts to a necklace. How clever! Unsigned, but looks like Avon. 1970s. $20.00 – 50.00. (Top right) Clip earrings. (Bottom right) Pierced earrings. Both pairs are unsigned, but look like Avon. 1970s. $15.00 – 35.00.

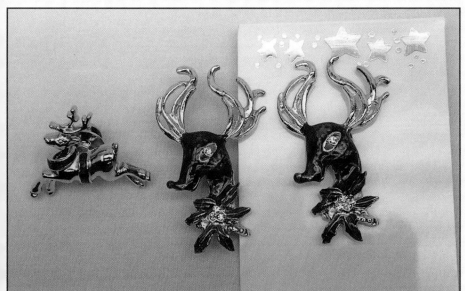

(Left) A rocking reindeer tac pin! Gold tone with a hint of red for the bridle. Signed "Avon." 1970s. $15.00 – 25.00. (Right) Highly detailed reindeer pins with bright red Rudolph noses. Gold with Christmas colors for the enameling and poinsettias used as bows. The reindeer on the right is still in the original package. 1¾". Unsigned. 1970s. $30.00 – 60.00.

(Left) Chic candlestick with white enameled body. Wax is dripping because the candle burns so hot! Red rhinestones are laced through the enameled pine needles. 2¼". Unsigned. 1960s. $30.00 – 50.00. (Right) Cuddly Mr. and Mrs. Snowman pin! A cozy, warm, creative pin set in a silver frame. The picture says it all. Back is silver. 1¾". 1950s. Unsigned. $55.00 – 85.00.

(Top) Santa pin and pierced earrings set. Chalk-like base with paint. 1¼" earrings, the pin measures one inch more. Early 1970s. Set: $20.00 – 40.00. (Bottom) Snowman pin and pierced earrings set. Chalk-like base and paint. Unsigned. $40.00 – 60.00.

(Left) Christmas angels. 1¾". Signed on the gold tag, "Made in China." Mid-1970s. $15.00 – 30.00. (Right) Pierced earrings and necklace set. Gold bells are suspended from a red, satin cord. Low budget. 16¾", necklace; 2¼", earrings. Unsigned. 1970s. For the set: $20.00 – 40.00.

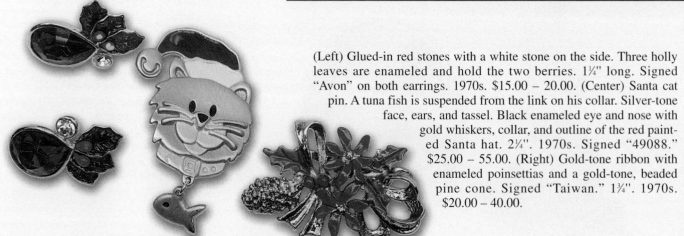

(Left) Glued-in red stones with a white stone on the side. Three holly leaves are enameled and hold the two berries. 1¼" long. Signed "Avon" on both earrings. 1970s. $15.00 – 20.00. (Center) Santa cat pin. A tuna fish is suspended from the link on his collar. Silver-tone face, ears, and tassel. Black enameled eye and nose with gold whiskers, collar, and outline of the red painted Santa hat. 2¼". 1970s. Signed "49088." $25.00 – 55.00. (Right) Gold-tone ribbon with enameled poinsettias and a gold-tone, beaded pine cone. Signed "Taiwan." 1¾". 1970s. $20.00 – 40.00.

(Left) Oh, the weather outside is frightful, but this pin is so delightful! This Christmas inspired wreath brooch has a red rhinestone glued in on the top of the bell. Small red, blue, and green cabochons are scattered about the leaves of the pin, with white enameling for the snow. 1¾" diameter. Unsigned. 1960s. $50.00 – 80.00. (Right) And since we've no place to go, let it snow, let it snow, let it snow! You'll be begging for snow when you wear this pin. This weighty pin has peridot topaz rhinestones and ruby cabochons splayed on the pin. Red, green, and white enameling complete the pin, and a red bow with a red center rhinestone is perched from the top. 1960s. $50.00 – 80.00.

Left) Gold-tone plating with red enameled bow with gold, reen, and red enameled beads surrounding the ringing ell, which is a small faux pearl. 1¾". Unsigned. 960s. $45.00 – 75.00. (Center) Circle sprig of win- er. Gold-tone plating. The gold circle embraces he sprig of emerald-colored rhinestones and a bow f small faux pearls. At the ends you will find a pea reen rhinestone. 1¾". Unmarked. Early 1960s. 40.00 – 50.00. (Right) The Christmas wreath pin as gold-tone plating and is very heavy. There are hree rows of holly with green and red enameled erries, also green enameling on the ribbon. 1½". Signed GERRYS©." 1960s. $60.00 – 80.00.

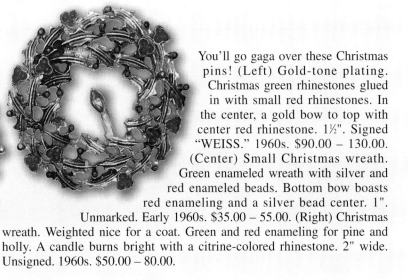

You'll go gaga over these Christmas pins! (Left) Gold-tone plating. Christmas green rhinestones glued in with small red rhinestones. In the center, a gold bow to top with center red rhinestone. 1½". Signed "WEISS." 1960s. $90.00 – 130.00. (Center) Small Christmas wreath. Green enameled wreath with silver and red enameled beads. Bottom bow boasts red enameling and a silver bead center. 1". Unmarked. Early 1960s. $35.00 – 55.00. (Right) Christmas wreath. Weighted nice for a coat. Green and red enameling for pine and holly. A candle burns bright with a citrine-colored rhinestone. 2" wide. Unsigned. 1960s. $50.00 – 80.00.

Rockin' around the Christmas trees! (Left) Gold-tone plating. Small red and green rhinestones decorate this tree. Red and green beads for tinsel, and an enameled star on top with a red rhinestone center. 1¾". Unmarked. 1960s. $45.00 – 65.00. (Center) I love this one! This pin is gold-tone plating. It's weighted and would look perfect on a heavy blazer. Glued-in stones for ornaments are open foiled backing. Small seed beads for trim. 2½". Unmarked. 1960s. $80.00 – 110.00. (Right) Gold-tone plating. Silver tone over the gold tree for a great tinsel look! Small red, green, and purple cabochons for the tree ornament, topped off with a small green rhinestone. 2". Unsigned. 1960. $45.00 – 65.00.

These svelte pieces would drive any woman wild. (Left) Christmas tree pin. Gold-tone plating. Reminds me of a simple true Christmas. Glued-in rhinestones for ornaments. A gold tree trunk and pot. 2¼". Unsigned. $20.00 – 30.00. An Avon Christmas tree pin, measures 2¼" long. The six gold electroplated bows have centers of aurora borealis stones. $40.00 – 80.00.

(Left) Christmas tree pin with red and green enameling for pine and ornaments, with open pines. A red enameled pot to finish. 2¼". Unsigned. 1960s to the 1970s. $40.00 – 60.00. (Center) A gold-tone plated Christmas tree pin with white enameling for snow. Green enameling is for the pine with three red enameled candy canes. The star topper includes a red rhinestone. 2½". Signed "©BJ." 1960s to the 1970s. $45.00 – 65.00. (Right) A weighty Christmas tree pin. Gold-tone plating. Green enameling and red for the ornaments topped off with a red enameled star. 2¼". ©BEARIX. $40.00 – 60.00.

(Left) This bell brooch is quite weighty. Gold-tone plating. Multicolored stones, glued-in green leaves that are detailed with small red stones, and one red stone on the ringer. ©BEATRIX. $90.00 – 130.00. (Right) This bell brooch is gold-tone plating. Christmas red and green over the silver-tone bells, with small pavè rhinestones for bell base and silver for the ringer. 2¼". Unsigned. $70.00 – 110.00.

Ring my bell, ring my bell! (Left) Gold-tone plating. This bell really rings! Green enameled leaves with a red cabochon. Holly tops off the bell. 1½". Unmarked. 1960s to early 1970s. $40.00 – 70.00. (Center) Gold-tone plating, and it really jingles, too! 2". Unmarked. 1960s. $45.00 – 75.00. (Right) Gold-tone plating. Dark green and red molded plastic for the holly trim. 1½" wide. Unmarked. Early 1970s. $30.00 – 50.00.

(Left) Candle pin of the 1960s. Ruby flame with white enameling for the wax. Base of gold with detailed holly and pine. 1½" long and 1¾" wide. $30.00 – 50.00. (Center) 2½" candle. Nice detail with the colors of the enameling. Small red rhinestones with one aurora borealis in the pine. 1960s. $30.00 – 50.00. (Right) 1¾" 1960s candle pin. Three pear-shaped ruby flames with a gold-tone base that has enameling for the wax and pine detail. All three of these are unsigned. Weighted. $30.00 – 50.00.

Indiana, Pennsylvania, is the Christmas tree capital of the world. (Left) 2¼" Christmas tree pin of the 1950s. Gold tone with colored stones for ornaments. Unsigned. $20.00 – 40.00. (Center) BEATRIX Christmas tree pin is 2½". Pin signed under the closure. Enameled over the gold tone in Christmas colors. Simple yet classic. 1960s. $30.00 – 50.00. (Right) 2½" Christmas tree pin is unsigned. This would be pretty on a coat. It is weighted. Pine is in 3-D with colored stones for the bulbs. $20.00 – 40.00.

(Left) Winter white pendant. 1" oval in a bezel setting. A delicate swirl border. Open backed. Unsigned. $50.00 – 80.00. (Center) Skater pin measures 2¼". Flexible bottom as this ice skater makes his moves. Gold-tone top with colored stones. Bottom is silver tone with colored stones. Skates, hands, and face are gold tone. Red enameled collar. Unsigned. Effective for the season! $45.00 – 75.00. (Right) Rockin' wreath of aurora borealis and seed pearls. 1960s. $25.00 – 45.00.

Screw-on earrings. Christmas bells. Two purple plastic beads are in the center of the bell. 1940s. Unsigned. $15.00 – 20.00.

(Left) Pin. Snow covered bells with pink beads in the center dangle from the Christmas bow. Dainty. Unsigned. 1940s. $10.00 – 15.00. (Right) Gold-tone bells, enameled red ringers, and green ivy. 1950s. $15.00 – 25.00.

Ringing in the season! (Left) Silver bells! Silver bells! These silver bells ring. They are suspended from the holly. In the center of the pine and holly is a red cabochon berry. Unsigned. Measures 2⅛". Pin from the 1950s. $25.00 – 45.00. (Right) Golden Christmas bell rings with the ringer. Berry and holly are enameled. 2". Pin is unsigned. 1950s. $20.00 – 30.00.

(Left) Poinsettia wreath pin from the 1960s. Enameling over metal. $25.00 – 45.00. (Right) This poinsettia Christmas pin is from the mid-1950s to the early 1960s. $35.00 – 55.00.

(Top) This bracelet is fun with all its Christmas fruit. 1960s. $30.00 – 50.00. (Bottom) Avon bracelet from the 1970s that slides. $25.00 – 45.00.

Miscellaneous

(Top) Light red plastic with a ruby rhinestone sternum. 1½". Late 1950s to mid-1960s. $30.00 – 50.00. (Center) White plastic flowers with topaz sternums. 1½". Unsigned. Late 1950s to mid-1960s. $30.00 – 50.00. (Bottom) My mother's clip earrings, though I've had them for awhile. Light orange plastic feathers with a single prong set aurora borealis stone. 2¾". Signed "Germany." Late 1950s to mid-1960s. Priceless.

Native, tropical! Barrel clasp, strung-on fishnet. Six gold beads are used to separate the brown beads. Measures 12⅛". Unsigned. $50.00 – 80.00.

Nicely faceted, amber colored glass beads. Hand strung on heavy string. 11¼". 1920s. Unsigned. $135.00 – 185.00.

Necklace is hand strung on heavy string. 8¾" long.
Unsigned. $65.00 – 105.00.

Tasteful necklace has banal clasp. Strung on fishnet.
Blues, purples, and bone in imitation bone. Super tropical! Unsigned. 11¾". $40.00 – 80.00.

11½". White glass beads with a swirl of cranberry through the
white. One bead is broken. Each bead measures 1". There are
22 beads with a barrel clasp to close. Unsigned. Early 1900s
to the teens. $225.00 – 265.00.

Clip-on earrings of the 1950s. These would be great with anyone's poodle skirt. Five pink plastic flowers with silver beads in the center. Unsigned. $15.00 – 25.00.

Signed "JAPAN." These clip-on earrings aren't mellow yellow! Plastic feathers make up these earrings. Notice the small rhinestones on the stems. $10.00 – 20.00.

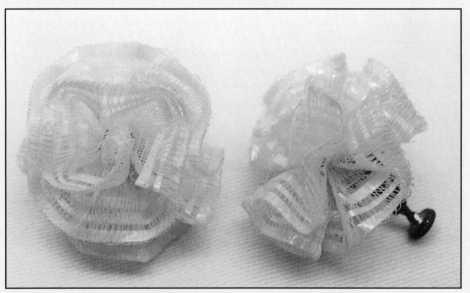

Unmarked screw-back earrings from the 1950s are done in 3-D. The white plastic flower is done in an open weave. $15.00 – 25.00.

A wonderful, bold, colorful 25" single strand of glass barrel beads strung on a fine wire. The beads are separated by six small glass beads. One blue bead is broken. Mid- to late 1900s. $180.00 – 230.00.

The 1950s were so nifty! This 17" single strand of heavy glass beads is strung tight. The beads are earthy tones and are separated by two gold-tone beads. Unsigned. $130.00 – 170.00.

Appealing colors with the faux pearls and coral-colored glass beads have great eye appeal. These are strung tight on a light string. Measures 7¾". Nice weight. Unmarked. From the late teens to the late 1920s. $95.00 – 135.00.

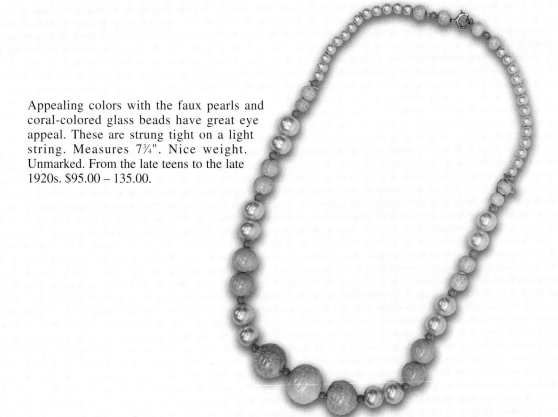

Heavy bracelet, early teens to the mid-1920s. The three charms look to be cornelian. A Greek design in the charm. Two charms measure ¾" with a center charm of 1". The bracelet is 8". Unmarked. $115.00 – 145.00.

Early 1900s bracelet of three gold-tone links with two Persian turquoise that are open backed. 6¾". Unmarked. $110.00 – 140.00.

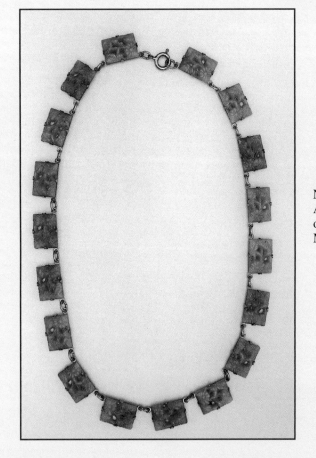

Necklace of "poor man's jade," commonly known as Peking glass. All are prong set by hand. Each linked by a silver ring. The back is open with a nicely detailed silver frame. Measures 7¾". Unsigned. Mid-teens to the early 1920s. $130.00 – 180.00.

1950s dazzling 14" single strand of plastic amber beads in three shapes. Each amber is separated by a black plastic bead. This is strung very tight on a double string. The barrel clasp is finished in amber so as not to distract from the necklace. $90.00 – 140.00.

1930s unmarked clip earrings. Great detail with a gold-tone turbine and large hoop earrings on the black face with defined red lipstick. To finish is a faux pearl under the chin. 1¼". $80.00 – 100.00.

Tag signed "1928," this is from the 1980s. A single strand of light blues, grays, and purples with silver metal beads to separate and a barrel clasp to close. Measures 17½". $45.00 – 85.00.

PAT 2066969 pin from the late 1920s. A celluloid man on a polished base in natural color. Measures 1½". $95.00 – 135.00.

Cufflinks signed "Swank" in the original gold velvet box. Heavy gold tone with purple cabochons in the center with a matching tie clasp. 1960s to 1970s. $75.00 – 105.00.

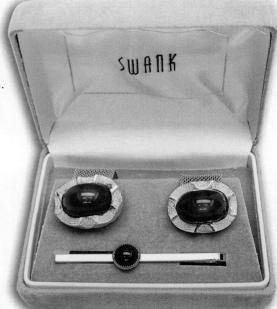

(Top) Defined craftsmanship for this mid-teens to 1920s brooch. It is unsigned and weighted. A variety of colors of glass oval stones with open backs. All are prong set by hand. Silver over metal in an open filigree design. Measures 2½". $120.00 – 150.00. (Bottom) Screw-back earrings. Mid-teens to the 1920s. Oval glass in topaz, aquamarine, and amethyst. The backs are open. Each is signed "Sterling." $60.00 – 90.00.

Signed "Swank." Gold tone. The initial "K" done in black with a silver center background. 1960s to 1970s. $50.00 – 90.00.

Signed "Swank." Gold tone. Diamond shaped with a rhinestone center. 1960s to the 1970s. $50.00 – 90.00.

All of these are from the 1960s to the 1970s. (Left) Unmarked, round silver-tone cufflink. $20.00 – 40.00. (Center) Signed "Swank." Open gold-tone square cufflink. $18.00 – 25.00. (Right) Unmarked, gold tone, with two engraved leaves. $20.00 – 30.00.

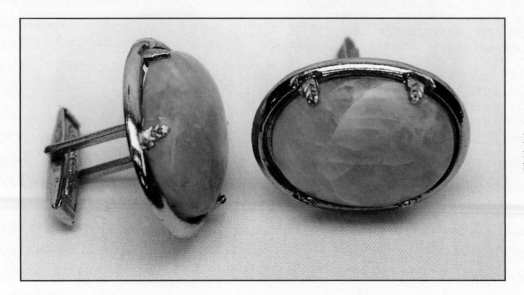

1960s to the 1970s. Signed "PAT PEND." Weighted silver-tone frame with prong set, open backed jadite. $50.00 – 90.00.

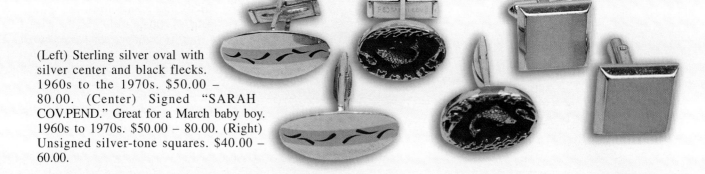

(Left) Sterling silver oval with silver center and black flecks. 1960s to the 1970s. $50.00 – 80.00. (Center) Signed "SARAH COV.PEND." Great for a March baby boy. 1960s to 1970s. $50.00 – 80.00. (Right) Unsigned silver-tone squares. $40.00 – 60.00.

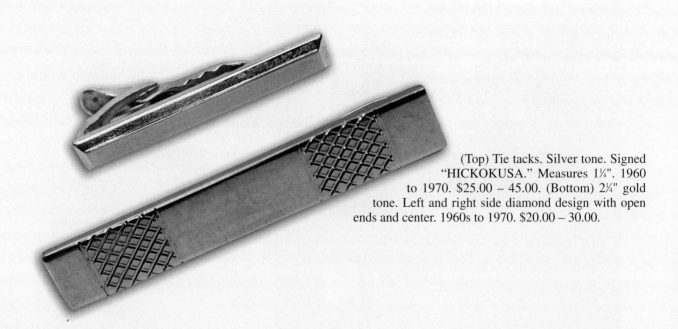

(Top) Tie tacks. Silver tone. Signed "HICKOKUSA." Measures 1¼". 1960 to 1970. $25.00 – 45.00. (Bottom) 2¼" gold tone. Left and right side diamond design with open ends and center. 1960s to 1970. $20.00 – 30.00.

(Top) W.E.H.CO. 2¼". Initials on front of the gold tone bar read "T E L." $30.00 – 60.00. (Center) Jaffa Shrine Pin $15.00 – 25.00. All of these are from the 1960s to 1970s. (Bottom) Gold-tone bar initials are "L L." 1¼". $25.00 – 45.00.

Mint green, lavaliere of the early 1900s to the late teens. 14". The pattern design is delicate. All beads are hand knotted on a heavy string. The drop string is unattached. The drop measures 3¾". Unmarked. $200.00 – 230.00.

(Top) ID Bracelet RUTHIE 1946. The back is stamped "STERLING ROLES." $30.00 – 60.00. (Bottom) The Lord's Prayer on brass to be worn on a chain. This measures 1¼". 1940s. No value assigned.

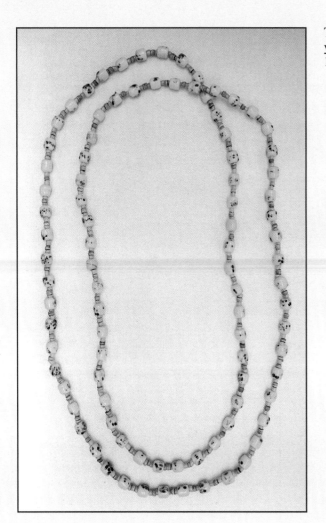

This is an adorable 23" necklace. Yellow beads separated by a small yellow bead, natural, then a yellow bead. Unsigned. Mid- to late 1900s. $170.00 – 230.00.

Very delicate state. Separated by a black bead. The center stone measures 2". Late 1800s to the mid-1910s. Unsigned. $250.00 – 325.00.

Unmarked single strand of glass beads in a variety of colors is hand strung on a heavy string. Measures 25½". The matching clip earrings are ¾". Mid- to late 1900s. $200.00 – 230.00.

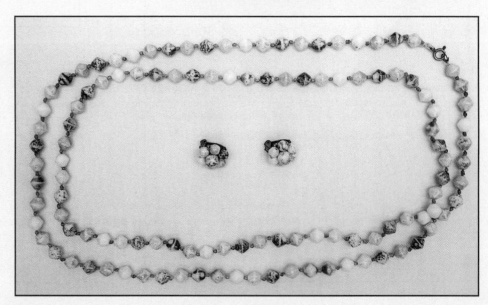

Lovely, unsigned necklace from the 1920s. Necklace has 9½" chain with a 2" drop, totaling 11½." Brilliant blue glass. $180.00 – 230.00.

2½" brooch that looks like it should convert to a pendant, but does not. 1900s to the early 1920s. Unsigned. $125.00 – 155.00.

Rocking ruby. The stone is set by hand. 1900s to the mid-1920s. Signed on top of the clasp, "1/20 14K." The rest is illegible. $210.00 – 290.00.

Such a delicate filigree frame for this necklace. Unsigned. Chain measures 9¾" and the stone is 1¾." $190.00 – 250.00.

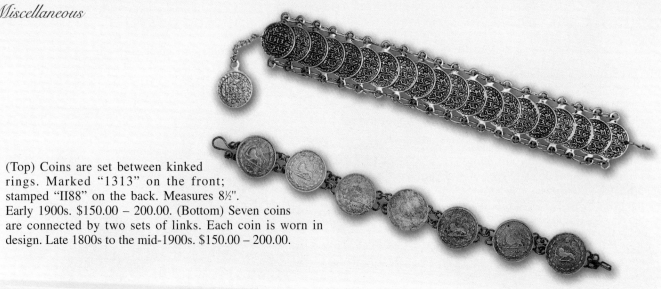

(Top) Coins are set between kinked rings. Marked "1313" on the front; stamped "II88" on the back. Measures 8½". Early 1900s. $150.00 – 200.00. (Bottom) Seven coins are connected by two sets of links. Each coin is worn in design. Late 1800s to the mid-1900s. $150.00 – 200.00.

(Top) Men's ring from the early 1930s. It is stamped "Sterling" and also "10K GOLD TOP." Nice ruby center with an open back. $130.00 – 180.00. (Bottom) Mother's ring. Seven birthstones in a range of colors. 1950s. $130.00 – 180.00.

Men's ring. Stamped "10K." Tiger's eye stone is engraved with what looks like two Greek soldiers. Early 1940s. $130.00 – 180.00.

(Left) Topical looking pin in a braided silver-tone frame. Signed "Made RM Italy." 1940s. $120.00 – 180.00. (Right) ¾" pin is a great color. Also, in great shape. Signed "Made in Italy." 1940s. $100.00 – 150.00.

Cool Copper

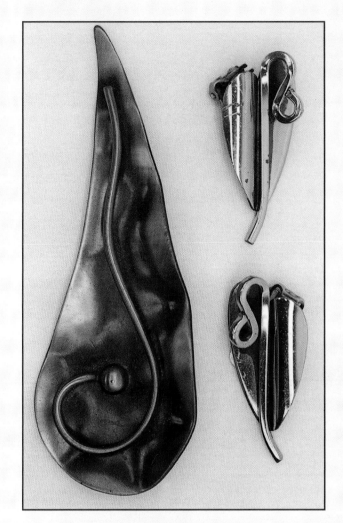

"There Is No Arizona." Remember the song? Southwest design for this unsigned copper necklace. The pendant measures 2" with the chain at 14¾". 1950s. $75.00 – 105.00.

(Top) Brooch is signed "GENUINE COPPER." Mid-1940s to the early 1950s. Measures 3¾". $100.00 – 130.00. (Bottom) Each of the clip earrings is signed "Renoir." Measures 1½". 1940s. $60.00 – 80.00.

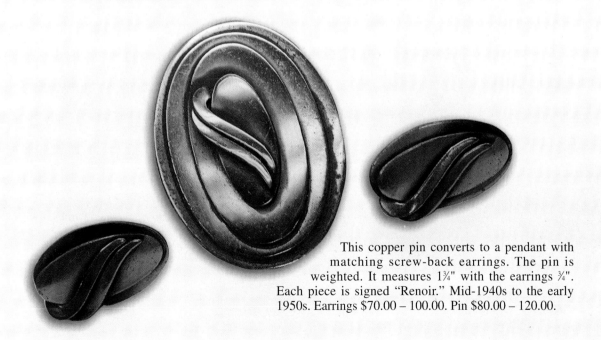

This copper pin converts to a pendant with matching screw-back earrings. The pin is weighted. It measures 1¾" with the earrings ¾". Each piece is signed "Renoir." Mid-1940s to the early 1950s. Earrings $70.00 – 100.00. Pin $80.00 – 120.00.

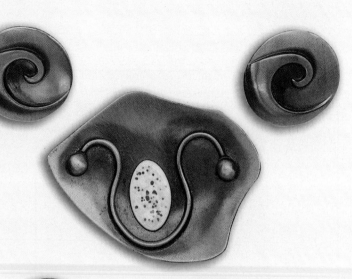

(Top) 1950s screw-on earrings in copper. Measure 1". $55.00 – 95.00. (Bottom) Brooch is signed "GENUINE COPPER." Copper with surface enamel oval in splash of green with white. Early 1950s. $90.00 – 130.00.

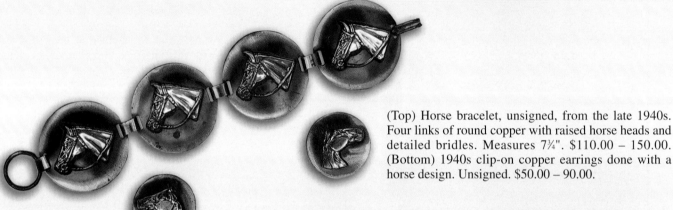

(Top) Horse bracelet, unsigned, from the late 1940s. Four links of round copper with raised horse heads and detailed bridles. Measures 7¾". $110.00 – 150.00. (Bottom) 1940s clip-on copper earrings done with a horse design. Unsigned. $50.00 – 90.00.

Bracelet and clip earrings that are weighted. This lovely copper bracelet has four links in two rows holding the Elizabeth II Regina coins. Measures 7¼". Matching earrings measure 1¼". 1940s. $110.00 – 150.00.

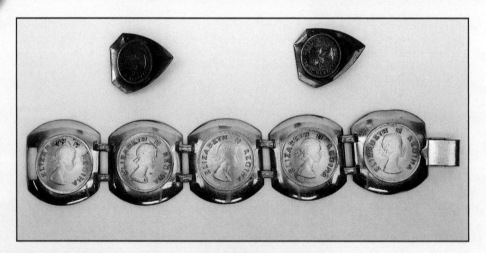

(Top) 7⅛" copper bracelet with seven rectangle links done in a Southwest design. Mid-1940s to the mid-1950s. $85.00 – 125.00. (Bottom) Ride 'em, cowgirl! A 7" copper bracelet with eight links in a design of a cowboy hat. Unsigned. Mid-1940s to the mid-1950s. $85.00 – 125.00.

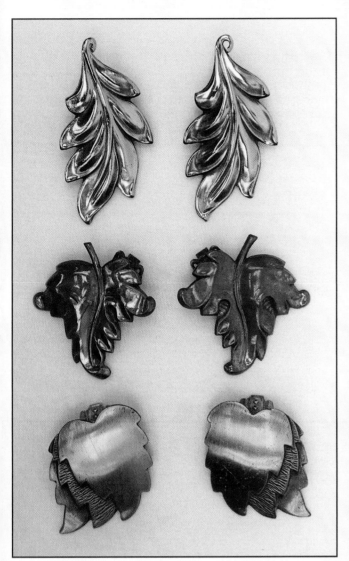

Looks like fall for all of these copper clip earrings. Mid-1940s to the mid-1950s. Each pair of earrings is detailed, showing quality craftsmanship. (Top) Measures 1¾". (Center) Measures 1¼". (Bottom) Measures 1¼". All pairs valued at $65.00 – 105.00.

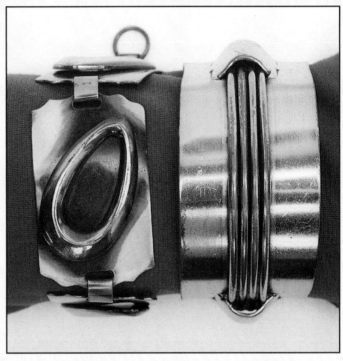

(Left) Super swirls. Unsigned. Copper. 1950s. $80.00 – 105.00. (Right) Cuff bracelet from the 1950s. Copper. Unsigned. $90.00 – 105.00.

1950s unsigned copper earrings. Measure 1½". The ¾" emerald stone is held by four prongs. $50.00 – 80.00.

Summertime Fun

(Top) A heavy 1950s expansion bracelet. Signed "JAPAN." White glass beads with silver tips. Bracelet is silver tone. $50.00 – 70.00. (Center) 1950s plastic expansion bracelet strung on double sets of heavy string. $30.00 – 40.00. (Bottom) Plastic expansion bracelet strung on a heavy nylon string. 1950s. $30.00 – 40.00.

(Outer) Men's cufflinks. Signed "Swank." Mother-of-pearl set between gold-tone bars. 1960s. $45.00 – 65.00. (Inner) Pin signed "Lisner" from the 1950s measures 1¾". The cabochons are open backed. Swirl of six plastic leaves in gold electroplate with a center gold-tone stem. $45.00 – 65.00.

(Top left) Signed Gerry's pin with four cream-enameled petals tipped with gold and a gold beaded center. Measures 1½". $45.00 – 75.00. (Top right) A pair of dainty flowers with aurora borealis in the center set on top of the gold-tone vine. Detail on the leaves looks bold. 3-D. $45.00 – 75.00. (Bottom left) Signed "TRIFARI," this pin is 2". White molded plastic set in metal with gold wash. $45.00 – 75.00. (Bottom right) Unmarked 2" floral pin. Winter white enameling over gold. $30.00 – 40.00. All of these pins are from the mid-1950s to the early 1960s.

(Top left) Signed "TRIFARI" pin measures 2¾". The back is brushed silver tone. Mid-1950s. $45.00 – 75.00. (Top right) 2¾" unsigned pin. The open wispy leaf has white paint over a gold tone. Late 1950s to the early 1960s. $20.00 – 30.00. (Bottom) Signed Lisner clip earrings from the mid-1950s. A center of four rhinestones held between silver bars. White enameled leaves on the outside. Measure 1⅛". $40.00 – 70.00.

(Top) Bracelet measuring 7¼" is unsigned. Gold electroplated with eight molded plastic squares. Double hoops to link this simple beauty. Late 1950s to the early 1960s. $40.00 – 60.00. (Bottom) 1950s bracelet. Unmarked. Measures 7⅛" with double strands. The white plastic is in a gold-tone bezel setting. $30.00 – 40.00.

Bracelet and clip earrings all signed "TRIFARI." White over gold tone, open lattice work. The bracelet is 6¾" and the earrings are 1". Mid-1950s to the early 1960s. $85.00 – 105.00.

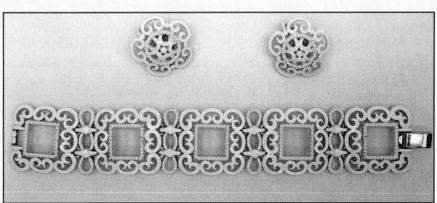

Choker signed "CORO." 8½" center with 8½" of adjustable chain with a fish-hook clasp. Caps done in gold tones show the ten nice white molded plastic squares. Style! 1960s. $75.00 – 100.00.

CORO parure. Gold-tone necklace, bracelet and clip earrings. White cabochon inflexible gold-tone brackets. Weighted set. Mid-1950s to the early 1960s. Measurements are: earrings 1¼", bracelet 7¼", and necklace 11¼", with a 5¼" adjustable chain with a fish-hook clasp. Bracelet is signed "CORO" on the clasp. Each clip is signed "CORO" as well as the fish-hook clasp on the necklace. A too hot to wear set, yet, this is one of my favorite sets for the heat of the summer! $155.00 – 185.00.

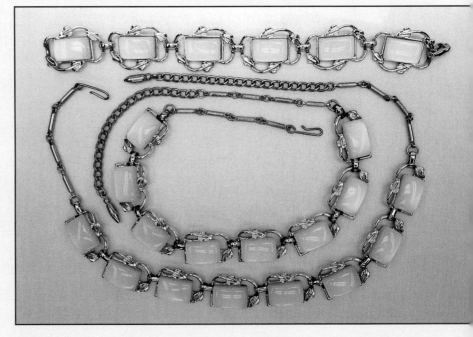

(Top) Bracelet is signed "CORO" on the clasp. Measures 7⅛". Six raised white plastic sets encompassed with an open gold-tone link design. Late 1950s. $40.00 – 70.00. (Bottom) You are not seeing double. This is a pair of chokers from the late 1950s. Looks like Coro, but they are unmarked. 8⅛" of chain and 9½" of adjustable chain. $50.00 – 80.00.

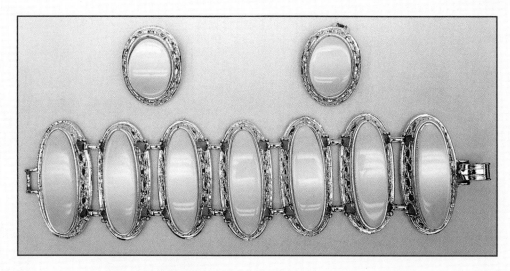

Matching clip earrings and bracelet, unmarked. Late 1950s. The bracelet measures 7¾" long and 2" wide. The earrings are 1¼" long. Winter white plastic with a gold-tone border. Closed backing. Striking! This set also would be great around the Christmas holiday season. $90.00 – 120.00.

(Top Left) Late 1950s clip earrings. Gold tone and multiple colors with four small aurora borealis set between leaves. One stone is missing. Signed "Lisner." $45.00 – 75.00. (Top right) Mid-1960s clip earrings. Coral color molded plastic sets in gold tone. Measure 1½". $30.00 – 40.00. (Center) Unmarked bracelet measuring 7¼". Three tones of molded plastic set in the gold-tone vines. Late 1950s. $45.00 – 75.00. (Bottom left) Signed "STAR" clip earrings. Two pea green maple leaves measure 1¼". Heavy. Late 1950s. $45.00 – 75.00. (Bottom right) Unmarked clip earrings. Late 1950s. Measure 1". Two buttercup oval cabochons in a horn of gold. $30.00 – 50.00.

Attractive CORO set! Bracelet has a safety chain and measures 6¾". The clasp is signed "CORO." Earrings are 1" with each clip being signed "CORO." The necklace is 7" at the center with 10½" of adjustable chain. Signed "CORO" on the fish-hook clasp. Gold-tone open weave surrounds the butter-colored cabochon squares with a hint of pastel confetti. Mid-1950s to the early 1960s. $150.00 – 180.00.

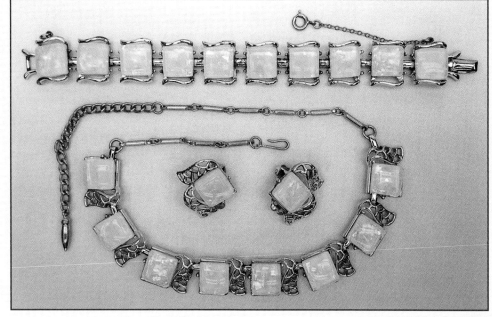

(Top) 7" bracelet done in silver over metal. Lilac molded plastic shells are open backed. The shells are topped off in lilac chaton rhinestones. Late 1950s. $40.00 – 60.00. (Bottom) Signed "Lisner" clip earrings. ¾" of a simple, yet stately design. In the center of the silver-tone circle is a cabochon amethyst. Mid-1960s. $45.00 – 75.00.

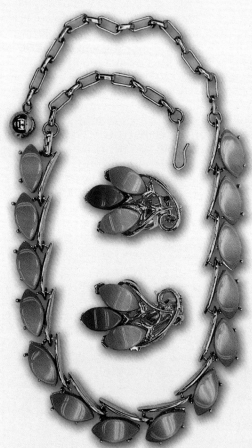

(Outer) Unsigned. Light purple marquee-shaped cabochons on a silver chain. The chain has a fish-hook clasp with a silver ball. 6½" long. 1950s. $110.00 – 160.00. (Inner) Clip earrings. Gray, blue, and aqua marquee cabochons, open backed. Silver tone. Unsigned. Measures 1¼", from the late 1950s. $30.00 – 50.00.

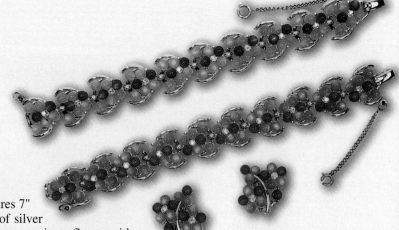

(Top) Bracelet. Late 1950s. Measures 7" and has a safety chain. Ten links of silver tone with blue cabochons in two-tone creating a flower with a center of aurora borealis glued in. Unsigned. $50.00 – 80.00. (Center) Ditto with the exception that this bracelet is pink. See top identification. (Bottom) 1" clip earrings from the late 1950s match the center bracelet. $60.00 – 80.00.

CORO, demi-parure. The chain of the necklace is 6¼" of adjustable chain with the center measuring 10". The drop is very stiff. All cabochons are closed backed. Bracelet is 7¼" with ten links of molded plastic. Signed on the safety chain. Colors of this set are greens and grays. Nicely detailed design of leaves with veins of three rhinestones on top of each leaf. Late 1950s. $130.00 – 150.00.

Coro, demi-parure choker and clip earrings. Earrings are 2" with each clip signed "CORO." The necklace is 9¼" of white beads on an adjustable chain. The center is 6¼" with two flowers on each side of the three. All are raised to create 3-D. Yellow petals are painted on plastic with gold borders and white centers. Mid-1950s. $115.00 – 145.00.

(Left) Pin. Faux ivory rose with a gold-tone stem. A leaf on each side. Mid-1960s to the early 1970s. Unmarked. 1¾". $40.00 – 60.00. (Right) Pin of faux ivory, signed "Lisner." Mid-1960s to the early 1970s. A single open leaf on the left of the rose. Measure 2¼". $50.00 – 70.00.

(Left) Signed "SARAH COV." Pin measures 1¾". Heavy braided rope in a double circle. Three gold-tone leaves hug the flower with a prong set jade. Complete with a stem with a faux pearl. Late 1960s to the mid-1970s. $75.00 – 105.00. (Right) Unmarked pin measures 1¾" with two faux ivory roses on a gold-tone stem. Enameled green plastic leaf on each side. Mid-1960s to the early 1970s. $40.00 – 60.00.

Necklace. 12¾". Hand strung on double string. The beads on each side of the necklace measure 5¼". Two sizes of leaves are in the center with a detailed vein. Sides have five leaves in overlay. Leaves in the center are separated by four beads. Heavy. 1970s. $105.00 – 135.00.

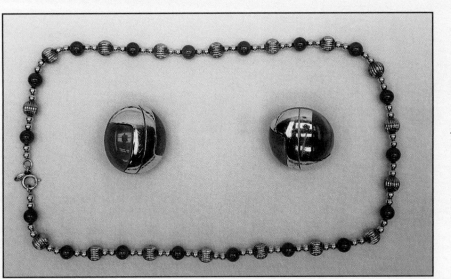

(Outer) Necklace. 8½". Signed on the clasp, "1/12KGF." The tag is signed "1/120 12KGFWRE." Two gold beads separate the jade, with a larger gold bead attached to the two small gold beads. Strung on wire. $110.00 – 150.00. (Inner) Clip earrings. Each clip is signed "LAVIN," 1970s. Weighted. Faux jade with two gold tone making one design in the center. $50.00 – 80.00.

(Left) 15" necklace. Fine chain link with ⅛" faux jade barrels hand painted. Unmarked. 1970s. $55.00 – 85.00. (Right outer) Necklace. 8⅛" fine gold-tone chain with four filigree gold-tone bars connected by a bead. Three jade are prong set and open backed. Signed "SORREN-TO STERLING." $110.00 – 150.00. (Right inner) ¾" clip earrings, unmarked. Bezel set green center has a carved leaf and flower design. Weighted. Mid-1940s to 1950s. Great detailing. These definitely deserve a second look. $75.00 – 95.00.

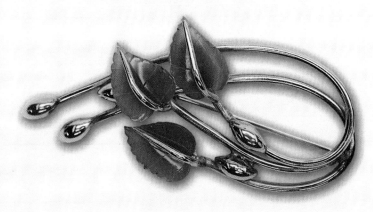

IRYA 2 WINARD 1/20 12kt gf. 1960s pin measures 2¼". Design is a vibrant gold-tone whirl wind with three jadeite leaves. $95.00 – 115.00.

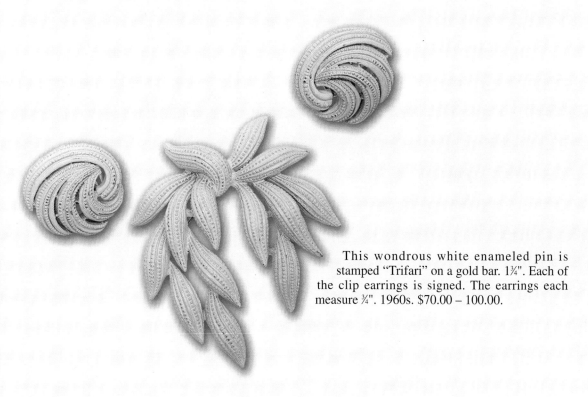

This wondrous white enameled pin is stamped "Trifari" on a gold bar. 1¾". Each of the clip earrings is signed. The earrings each measure ¾". 1960s. $70.00 – 100.00.

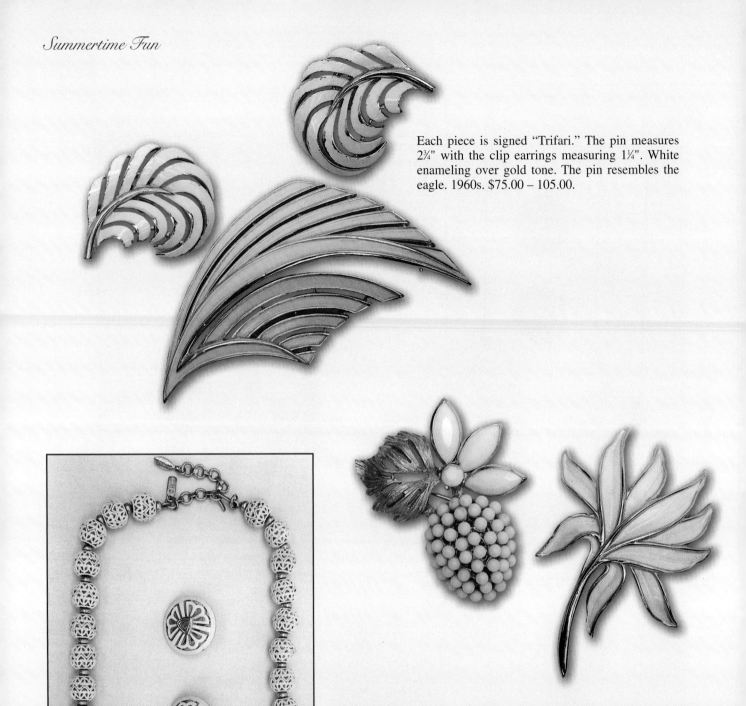

Each piece is signed "Trifari." The pin measures 2¾" with the clip earrings measuring 1¼". White enameling over gold tone. The pin resembles the eagle. 1960s. $75.00 – 105.00.

These two beauties are such the reminder of summertime. (Left) BSK pineapple measures 2". 1960s. $50.00 – 80.00. (Right) Trifari white enameling over gold tone. This pin is almost tropical. 1960s. $50.00 – 80.00.

Necklace with tag stamped "Monet." 7¼" adjustable chain and 2¾" fishhook clasp. Late 1960s. $70.00 – 100.00. The necklace's matching clip earrings were not photographed. The earrings in the center are marked "Trifari" and are from the 1960s. $25.00 – 45.00.

(Top) Plastic clip butterflies with aurora borealis. 1950s. $30.00 – 50.00. (Bottom) Cute flowers signed "Made in West Germany." $35.00 – 55.00.

(Top left) 2⅛" flag pin. 1960s to the 1970s. Rocking red, white, and blue rhinestones. $35.00 – 65.00. (Bottom center) Happy hoops. Red and white rhinestones in loops that are hooked together. 1960s. 1¾". $40.00 – 70.00. (Top right) Lisner red, white, and blue pin from the 1960s. Seven stones are missing. 2¼." $50.00 – 90.00.

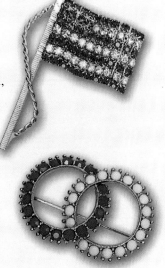

In honor of the 1976 Bicentennial, both pieces are priceless. I know the owner wore both heavily. I am so proud of the United States military! $35.00 – 65.00. (Left) Spirit of '76 necklace. 2¼" with 11½" silver tone chain. Signed "Cinerama Cranstan©, RI." Stamped on the bottom. 1970s. (Right) Necklace. Reads, "Proclaim liberty through out all the land." The back is nicely detailed. Pendant is 1¾" and the chain is 12½." 1970s. $35.00 – 65.00.

Banging butterfly pin. Yellow and black enameling over metal. 3⅛." Unsigned. 1960s. $45.00 – 85.00.

(Top) Mother pin made from plastic. (Bottom) Mother pin made from mother-of-pearl. The dangling star holds a small blue stone. The pin is marked "Skyline Drive." Each banner pin is from the 1950s and measures 1½" wide. $50.00 – 90.00.

All pins are unmarked, except the bottom left, which reads, "AUUA Made in Taiwan." Not your ordinary, garden variety array of butterflies. All from the 1960s; all enameling over metal. Prices range from $20.00 – 45.00. The bottom center bumblebee is enameling over silver tone metal. 1960s. Unsigned. $25.00 – 35.00.

(Left) 1950s scatter turtle pins in gold tone with marbleized cabochons for backs. Measures 1¼" and is signed "Gerry's." $70.00 – 105.00. (Center) A 1950s seahorse signed "ORNK." Measures 2⅛". $80.00 – 110.00. (Top right) ½" unmarked ladybug scatter pins from the 1950s. These are my least favorite bugs. $40.00 – 70.00. (Bottom right) 1½" signed "BURT 1/20 12K GF Cassell." From the 1960s. Two owls, made of tiger's eye, rest atop the gold-tone twig with gold-tone tails. $75.00 – 105.00.

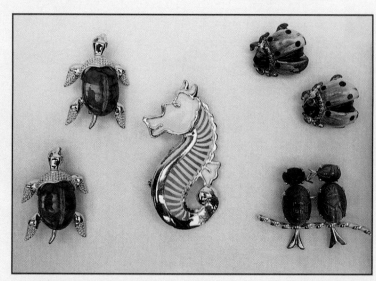

Personalizing Jewelry

This chapter will help to determine what type of jewelry one should wear according to face shape, complexion, eye color, and hair shade.

First, let's determine your face shape. The four shapes are: square, round, oblong, and heart.

A square face is straight with a squared forehead. The cheekbones and jaw line are the same width; the jaw is the dominant feature. You look your best if you select a necklace that is in the shape of a "V." Wear round shapes at the throat that will soften the square jaw line. Chokers with a circle design are also a fine accent for you. I suggest that you choose oval and round brooches, pins, and earrings. Rounded and soft-edged pieces complement you.

A round face is as wide as it is long with a short chin, soft rounded jaw line, and hairline. You look your best if you select long lengths in necklaces or necklaces that end in the shape of a "V." Wear shapes that cause the eye to move vertically. These would be angular or geometric, which are square or diamond design. I suggest that you choose dangle earrings in an angular design; pieces that add length will flatter you.

A narrow jaw with an angular chin and shallow temple with a high forehead make an oblong-shaped face. You look your best if you select oval or round beads or chain link necklaces. Wear circular or swirl designs which will add width to your eye area. I suggest that you choose short necklaces or chokers to reduce the length of the face. Horizontal-shaped pieces add width to your face. This makes for quite a stunning accent!

The heart-shaped face has a prominent cheekbone. The face is wide at the temple and forehead with a tapered narrow chin and jaw line. You look your best if you select round and square-shaped beads. Wear earrings that are wider at the bottom. Dangles and hoops complement you, too. Pieces adding width to the chin line give you elegance.

Suggestions to complement your skin tone, eye coloring, and hair coloring:

Dark and olive complexions should wear bronze toned metals.
Pale complexions become vibrant with red jewelry.
Tan complexions are bronzed with whites in earrings, necklaces, and bracelets.
Warm complexions are glowing in golds, bronzes, coppers, and lighter colored rhinestones.

Hair:

Blondes should have fun wearing gold, coral, and pearls.
Brunettes do best with pearls, silver, burgundy, and garnets.
Grey is gorgeous with silver and platinum.
Auburn is amazing with amber, tiger's-eye, and gold.

Eyes:

Blue is becoming with aquamarines, lapis, and sapphires.
Brown is bright with tiger's-eye, amber, topaz, and amethyst.
Green is grand with emeralds, hazel tones, and jade.

Care of Costume Jewelry

Do not spray perfume or oils on your jewelry.

If you store jewelry in plastic bags, this will enable the jewelry to resist moisture. Wrap loosely and store in boxes, drawers or plastic containers. If displayed in an open area, cover with a soft cloth that will not catch the prongs.

Do not place the jewelry close together. This can shift the prongs and loosen the stones.

Like glassware, extreme heat and cold creates damage. Changing environments may also affect the jewelry.

When storing earrings, place them on earring holders, if possible. If not, lay them flat. Bracelets and necklaces should be flat with stones turned upward.

Do not place the jewelry in water. If water is between the stone and backing, it can tarnish the stone. Gently clean with a Q-tip and glass cleaner, watching that the prongs do not catch. Depending on the piece, you may want to use dishwashing soap. Then use a jeweler's cloth or a soft cloth to polish.

Remove jewelry before sports, swimming in salt water, etc.

Use a jeweler's cloth to buff.

Store the jewelry so the pieces are not rubbing against each other.

Store in an area that is not damp. Weather can ruin the finish, and extreme heat or cold can loosen the stones.

Displaying Jewelry

Daring to display your jewelry shows just how creative you can be. This is where you can enjoy and have fun with your collection.

Mirrors can do wonders for costume jewelry. Get creative.

Frames.

Glass top coffee tables.

Hang on windows so they can catch the light.

If you have any mounts that allow you to display your pieces, this can be a fun way to show off your prized possessions.

Jewelry can be pinned to, or hung on, pillows, dolls, stuffed animals and lampshades.

Pictoral Review, October 1923.

Saturday Evening Post, February 26, 1946

Life, May 5, 1952

TV LEADING LADIES CONTINUED

GRACE IS GAY AT THE START OF HER TELECAST

A slender-stemmed blonde
from a famous Kelly clan

Until she began acting in TV two years ago, 22-year-old Grace Kelly was more famous for her relatives than for her long-stemmed, blonde beauty or her acting talent. Her father and her brother were both champion oarsmen. One uncle, George Kelly, is a noted playwright (*Craig's Wife*). Another uncle, Walter C. Kelly, was the famous "Virginia Judge" of vaudeville.

Grace came to New York five years ago to study acting and got some training in summer stock. Her TV plays have ranged from *Berkeley Square* to F. Scott Fitzgerald's *The Rich Boy*. In one hectic 13-day period she played three roles: a college girl on Tuesday, a rich girl on Sunday and, eight days later, a country school-teacher. Usually cast as a wholesome ingenue, she was happily surprised a few weeks ago to find herself on *Lights Out* playing a provocative music hall singer in short skirts and black mesh stockings (*right*). Her TV performances have brought Hollywood offers and last year she played in *High Noon* opposite Gary Cooper. But her first love has always been Broadway. Last week her ambitions were gratified when she opened in a play called *To Be Continued*. The show's reviews were so poor, however, that Miss Kelly will probably be back on TV soon.

142

AS A MUSIC HALL GIRL WHO DRIVES MEN TO MURDER, GRACE KELLY MAKES A QUICK CHANGE

Life, May 5, 1952

Jewels specially selected for Mother's Day. From upper left, reading clockwise: "Lorelei" Necklace, **$7.50**, Earrings $4, Bracelet (not shown) $4. "Spring Fantasy" Necklace $7.50, Bracelet $10, Earrings $5, Pin $7.50. (Also with Lilac, Jonquil, or Mock-diamond stones.) "Park Avenue Zoo" Charm Pins; Poodle, Lady Bug, Frog; (not shown) Elephant, Horseshoe, Duck, $3 each. "Enchanted Garden" Pin $6, Earrings $4. "Camellias" Pin $5, Necklace $5, Earrings $3, Bracelet $7.50. **Plus Tax.**

Life, May 5, 1952

Good Housekeeping, November 1952

Good Housekeeping, November 1952

Life, March 21, 1955

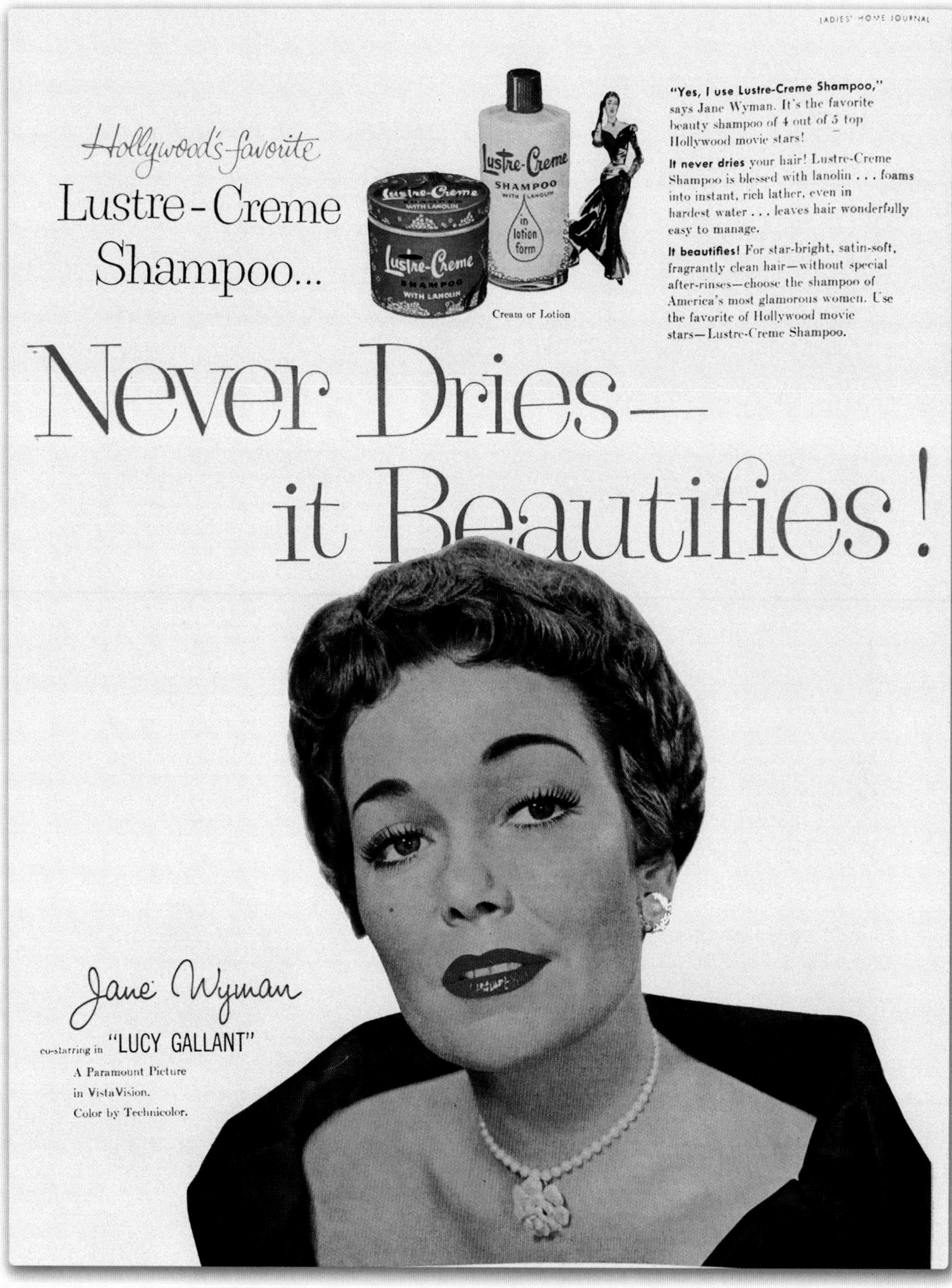
LADIES' HOME JOURNAL
Hollywood's favorite
Lustre-Creme Shampoo...
Lustre-Creme SHAMPOO WITH LANOLIN
Lustre-Creme SHAMPOO
in lotion form
Cream or Lotion
"Yes, I use Lustre-Creme Shampoo," says Jane Wyman. It's the favorite beauty shampoo of 4 out of 5 top Hollywood movie stars!
It never dries your hair! Lustre-Creme Shampoo is blessed with lanolin . . . foams into instant, rich lather, even in hardest water . . . leaves hair wonderfully easy to manage.
It beautifies! For star-bright, satin-soft, fragrantly clean hair—without special after-rinses—choose the shampoo of America's most glamorous women. Use the favorite of Hollywood movie stars—Lustre-Creme Shampoo.
Never Dries—
it Beautifies!
Jane Wyman
co-starring in "LUCY GALLANT"
A Paramount Picture
in VistaVision.
Color by Technicolor.

Ladies Home Journal, May 1955

Ladies' Home Journal, May 1955

Anne Patton, busy wife and mother of four children, looks as pretty as a picture (above), because she devotes intelligent planning to every aspect of her life.

Fresh accessories, a perfume you love, help create a party mood.

Prescription for Beauty:
a husband who helps; well-behaved children

By *DAWN CROWELL NORMAN* *Beauty Editor of the Journal*

Try a leisurely breakfast to help you start the day cheerfully.

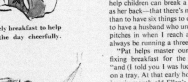

Do your vegetable preparing or mending out in the sunshine.

"THERE are plenty of things to frazzle and exhaust you when you have four children under the age of eight to care for," says pretty Anne Patton. "I know, for instance, that irritable, won't-help children can break a mother's spirits as well as her back—that there's nothing more frustrating than to have six things to do all at once. I'm lucky to have a husband who understands this, and who pitches in when I reach a bottleneck so I won't always be running a three-ring circus!

"Pat helps master our morning situation by fixing breakfast for the children," says Anne, "and (I told you I was lucky!) he brings me mine on a tray. At that early hour I'm apt to be changing six-month-old Ellen's diaper or sorting socks. But eating breakfast upstairs where I have a chance to relax and enjoy it is a peaceful way to start the day. Later, when Pat comes home from work, he gives me a hand with the children. And he's cheerful about doing it. He doesn't make me feel he's taking over *my* job!"

Irritable, balky children who haven't learned to help themselves can shatter a mother's nerves and cause her real fatigue. This is a situation the Pattons rarely come up against, but not by chance. "Pat is the main provider of the kind of *consistent*, firm-but-gentle discipline that sinks into little heads!

"All the children are being trained to pick up after themselves and keep their rooms tidy. These chores don't always go off without a hitch. But by encouraging (or insisting when necessary) that they carry out their jobs, Pat and I believe the children are getting an invaluable lesson in self-sufficiency. And their efforts lighten my work."

Even the busiest household schedule should allow time for a mother to get some rest. Five-minute periods of complete relaxation at odd times during the day can work wonders in renewing strength and brightening your outlook! Anne Patton considers her hour's nap each day her biggest beauty treatment. "It's CONTINUED ON PAGE 161

Young
HOW AMERICA LIVES

Regular exercise will keep your body fit and firm, your spirits high.

When papa helps he's rewarded with a more appreciative mate.

DRAWINGS BY MCCULLOUGH

Ten minutes in a tub of warm water and suds soothes, scents and relaxes.

Ladies' Home Journal, June 1955

Ladies' Home Journal, July 1956

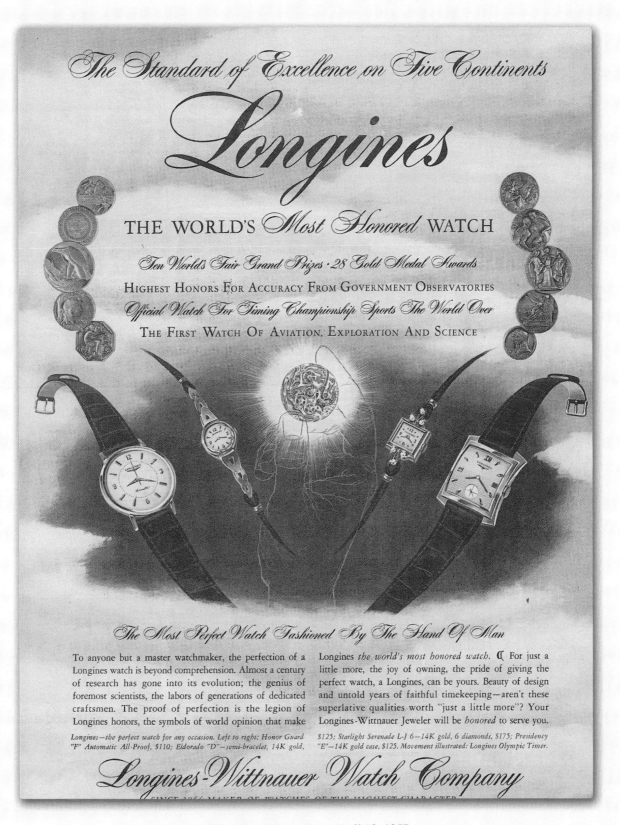

she can't see a thing but *jewels by* TRIFARI

(A) SOUTH SEAS Necklace 5.00, Bracelet 5.00, Earrings 3.00.
(B) ALLURE Necklace 10.00, Bracelet 10.00, Earrings 7.50.
(C) SANTA ANITA Necklace 6.00, Bracelet 5.00, Earrings 3.00.
(D) EBBTIDE Pin 5.00, Earrings 4.00.
(E) SYNCOPATION Necklace 6.00, Bracelet 5.00, Earrings 4.00.
(F) SPRING FROST Pin 7.50, Earrings 7.50.
(G) GARDEN PARTY Large Earrings 6.00.
(H) WHITE GARLAND Earrings 4.00.
(J) GARDEN PARTY Necklace 7.50,
Bracelet 7.50, Earrings 4.00.
(K) DOUBLOON Earrings 3.00,
Prices plus tax,
Not authentic unless stamped TRIFARI.
Jewelry designs copyrighted.

©1957 TRIFARI

You...terrific in turquoise

You...beautiful in beige

Angel Face makes all the difference. Left: Blushing Angel Face. Right: Tan Angel Face. Select <u>your</u> correct shades from the chart below.   Eyes by Aziza

Pond's new *Angel Face* with <u>cosmetic-silicones</u> lets you change your skin tone to look lovely in any fashion color

Here's the first fashion cosmetic—Pond's new Angel Face! It's the *only* compact makeup with cosmetic-silicones that actually lets you wear different skin tones for different fashion colors!

You can choose an Angel Face shade to brighten your skin . . . another to lighten . . . another to tone down your complexion. Angel Face makes hard-to-wear fashion colors flattering to you as no other makeup can. Because Angel Face—and no other makeup—has cosmetic-silicones.

This Pond's discovery lets Angel Face change your skin tone naturally, beautifully. Cosmetic-silicones form a protective barrier against skin moisture so Angel Face shades won't darken or discolor . . . will conceal tiny freckles and flaws. Build yourself a fabulous fashion reputation! Today, buy two, three or more new Angel Face shades and look lovely in *any* fashion color!

Beautiful new Fashion Case holds the finest powder and foundation in-one. Black or white with 24k gold design $1.25. New aqua Vanity Case for home or purse 69¢. Both plus tax.

Pond's costume-complexion coordinator				
costume colors	fair skin	rosy skin	olive skin	dark olive
	POND'S ANGEL FACE SHADES			
reds-pinks	ivory	natural	natural	tawny
oranges-yellows	golden	golden	golden	bronze
greens-blues	natural	ivory	pink	blushing
browns-black	pink	ivory	blushing	tawny
white-neutrals	natural	tawny	blushing	tan or deep tan

Saga

Gina Lollobrigida, Italy's prettiest export, is not satisfied with mere beauty. She wants to be admired for her acting too.

As far as can be determined, the first time Gina Lollobrigida was ever seen by an American, she was hiding in an empty wine vat. She was fourteen then, dirty and half-starved, and her discoverer was one of Gen. Mark Clark's G.I.'s. Fleeing north ahead of the tide of battle in Italy in 1944, the Lollobrigida family had taken refuge in the cellar of a gutted house along the road from Rome to Florence. Here the Americans—and peace—overtook them.

Since that time, life has changed a good deal for Gina. Today, at thirty-one, she is among the most popular movie actresses in Europe and well on her way to duplicating the feat in this country. Americans have already seen her in such pictures as *Trapeze* in 1956, an ill-fated remake of *The Hunchback of Notre Dame* in 1957, and in *Solomon and Sheba* and *Never So Few*, both released late last year—and they are due to see a lot more of her in the

Modest Gina objects to costumes such as this one, which the producers made her wear in *Solomon and Sheba*.
Below, Gina sight-seeing in Acapulco, Mexico, during the filming of *Go Naked in the World*.

Saturday Evening Post, August 13, 1960

# of a Siren

By ROBERT JOHNSON

Dr. Milko Skofic gave up his medical practice nine years ago to manage his wife Gina's career. Their son, Milko Jr., is three.

near future. During the years since 1944, moreover, her face has launched more admiring adjectives than ever-Helen's did ships, for *Signorina* Lollobrigida—pronounced "Lo-lo-bridge-i-da," with the accent on "bridge"—is unquestionably one of the world's most beautiful women.

Standing only five feet four inches, Gina in the flesh is quite surprisingly smaller than she appears on the screen, and the almost perfect hourglass shape into which her 118 pounds are poured is dainty rather than robust. Considering her statistical measurements of 36½-22-36, however, it is hardly surprising that film critics seldom fail to comment on Gina's figure, and more particularly on her bosom. Even the sedate (Continued on Page 74)

Gina played the gypsy girl in the poorly received *Hunchback of Notre Dame*. Mindful of her appeal as a pin-up girl, Gina yearns to be acknowledged as a dramatic actress. Her first serious acting effort, *Go Naked in the World*, will be released early next year.

1948, Derry Township prom, Lou and Dee Iezzi. Note Dee's jewelry. Today Mr. and Mrs. Iezzi reside near me.

Glossary

Aurora Borealis – Colors ranging from pale reds to yellows to a deep red color. Also known as Lumen Borealis; northern twilight popular as the northern lights. Rhinestones are treated with metals to provide the aurora color.

Baguette – A rectangular, narrow shaped stone.

Bakelite – A phenol formaldehyde resin. Bakelite was available in many colors. Bakelite was used in the production of costume jewelry, accessories, and household products.

Base Metal – A metal of a low value. Types of base metal are as follows: Brass — an alloy of copper and zinc, Pinch back — copper, tin and zinc that resembles gold, White metal — has an appearance of pewter and silver; also known as Pot metal.

Bezel setting – A set stone that is held securely by metal flanges embracing the stone.

Cabochan – An unfaceted stone that is most likely round or oval and merely polished without being cut into facets.

Chaton – A popular cut in round stones found in costume jewelry.

Celluloid – An early plastic that was used in hair accessories, dresser sets, and costume jewelry.

Chromium – A shiny, hard and brittle metal. A grayish white metallic that does not rust easily.

Electroplate – Process of fusing metals of different qualities.

Enamel – Process of melting a glasslike substance and then cooling it to make a smooth hard surface. Painting and varnishing the smooth surface in costume jewelry.

Emerald Cut – A square cut stone.

Faux – Not genuine, fake, or false.

Filigree – A decorative pattern made of wires and done in open work.

Gilding – An application of gold onto a surface of another object produced from another material.

Hand set – Stones that are placed individually in the metal setting.

Japanned – A process which colors metals to a dull black.

Jet – Coal with a high polish used in jewelry.

Lavalliere – A thin chain with a single suspended drop or stone. May be spelled lavaliere.

Marked – When a manufacture's or designer's identifying mark is stamped, carved, or signed into the jewelry.

Parcel-gilt – Silver objects which have been somewhat enriched with gilding.

Parure – Set of matched jewelry.

Paste – Imitation rhinestones or diamonds.

Patina – A green rust that occurs on jewelry and other metals when they hold a high bronze or copper content.

Pavè – Setting of stones placed together closely so no metal is showing.

Pear cut – Cut in the shape of a tear or a pear.

Prystal – Plastic substitute imitating glass.

Retro – Back, behind, and prior. Already used in the past and will be used in the future.

Rhinestone – An imitation diamond, made of glass.

Rhodium – An extremely hard and brittle metal with a white color and a metallic luster. Looks like platinum. Founded in 1803 among grains of crude platinum.

Signed – When a manufacture's or designer's identifying mark or signature is etched, carved, or stamped into the jewelry.

Tapered Baguettes – Narrow, rectangular shape that is large at one end and tapers downward to a smaller size.

Unsigned or Unmarked – Jewelry that was not stamped, carved, or etched by the designer or manufacturer.

White metal – A mix of zinc, lead, and tin with cadmium.

Bibliography

Aswad & Weinstein. *The Art & Mystique of Shell Cameos*. Florence, AL: Books Americana, 1991.

Avon pamphlet, (c) 1993. Avon Products, Inc.

Baker, Lillian. *Art Nouveau & Art Deco Jewelry An Identification & Value Guide*. Paducah, KY: Collector Books, 1981.

_____. *Fifty Years of Collectible Fashion Jewelry 1925 – 1975*. Paducah, KY: Collector Books, 1986.

_____. *100 Years of Collectible Jewelry An Identification and Value Guide*. Paducah, KY: Collector Books, 1978.

Bell, Jeanenne. *Answers to Questions About Old Jewelry 1840 – 1950 2nd Edition*. Florence, AL: Books Americana, 1985.

Brown, Marcia. *Signed Beauties of Costume Jewelry Volume II Identification and Values*. Paducah, KY: 2004.

_____. *Unsigned Beauties of Costume Jewelry Identification and Values*. Paducah, KY: Collector Books, 2000.

Bruton, LaRee Johnson. *Ladies Vintage Accessories Identification and Value Guide*. Paducah, KY: Collector Books, 2001.

Dolan, Maryanne. *Collecting Rhinestone Colored Jewelry An Identification & Value Guide 2nd Edition*. Florence, AL: Books Americana, 1989.

_____. *Collecting Rhinestone and Colored Jewelry An Identification & Value Guide 3rd Edition*. Florence, AL: Books Americana, 1993.

Edeen, Karen L. *Vintage Jewelry for Investment and Casual Wear*. Paducah, KY: Collector Books, 2002.

Gallina, Jill. *Christmas Pins Past and Present Second Edition*. Paducah, KY: Collector Books, 2004.

Henzel, Sylvia S. *Collectible Costume Jewelry Revised Edition*. Radnor, PA: Wallace-Homestead.

_____. *Collectible Costume Jewelry Id & Value Guide 3rd Edition*. Iola, WI: Krause Publications.

Kaplan, Arthur Guy. *Offical Price Guide to Antique Jewelry*. New York, NY: Random House, 1990.

Leshner, Leigh. *Rhinestone Jewelry A Price And Identification Guide*. Iola, WI: Krause Publications, 2003.

_____. *Vintage A Price Guide and Identification Guide 1920s – 1940s*. Iola, WI: Krause Publications, 2002.

Marsh, Madeleine. *Miller's Collectibles Price Guide*. Heron Quay's, London: Octopus Publishing Group LTD. 1999.

Miller, Harrice Simmons. *Costume Jewelry Official Identification & Price Guide First Edition*. New York, NY: Random House, 1990.

_____. *Costume Jewelry The Confident Collector 2nd Edition*; New York, NY: Avon, 1994.

Remero, Christie. *Warman's Jewelry Encyclopedia of Antique and Collectibles*. Radnor, PA: Wallace-Homestead Book Company, 1995.

Rivers, Joan. *Jewelry By Joan Rivers*, New York, NY: Abbeyville Press, 1995.

Schiffer, Nancy and Lyngerda Kelly. *Costume Jewelry the Great Pretenders Revised 4th Edition*. Atglen, PA: RE- 2002.

Simonds, Cherri. *Collectible Costume Jewelry*. Paducah, KY: Collector Books, 1997.

Smith, Pamela. *Price Guide to Vintage Fashion and Fabrics*. New York, New York: House of Collectibles, 2001.

Snell, Doris J. *Antique Jewelry with Prices*. Radnor, PA: Wallace-Homestead Book Company, 1984.

Tait, Hugh. *Jewelry 7,000 Years*. New York, NY: Harry N. Abrams, Incorporated, 1987.

informing today's collector

COLLECTOR BOOKS

GLASSWARE & POTTERY

4929	**American Art Pottery**, 1880 – 1950, Sigafoose	$24.95
6321	**Carnival Glass**, The Best of the Best, Edwards/Carwile	$29.95
6344	Collectible **Vernon Kilns**, Nelson	$29.95
6327	Collector's Encyclopedia of **Depression Glass**, 16th Ed., Florence	$19.95
5748	Collector's Encyclopedia of **Fiesta**, 9th Ed., Huxford	$24.95
5609	Collector's Encyclopedia of **Limoges Porcelain**, 3rd Ed., Gaston	$29.95
1358	Collector's Encyclopedia of **McCoy Pottery**, Huxford	$19.95
5677	Collector's Encyclopedia of **Niloak**, 2nd Edition, Gifford	$29.95
5678	Collector's Encyclopedia of **Nippon Porcelain**, 6th Series, Van Patten	$29.95
5618	Collector's Encyclopedia of **Rosemeade Pottery**, Dommel	$24.95
5842	Collector's Encyclopedia of **Roseville Pottery**, Vol. 2, Huxford/Nickel	$24.95
5921	Collector's Encyclopedia of **Stangl Artware**, Lamps, and Birds, Runge	$29.95
5680	Collector's Guide to **Feather Edge Ware**, McAllister	$19.95
6124	Collector's Guide to **Made In Japan Ceramics**, Book IV, White	$24.95
6559	**Elegant Glassware** of the Depression Era, 11th Edition, Florence	$24.95
5261	**Fostoria Tableware**, 1924 – 1943, Long/Seate	$24.95
6320	Gaston's **Blue Willow**, 3rd Edition	$19.95
5899	**Glass & Ceramic Baskets**, White	$19.95
6127	The **Glass Candlestick** Book, Vol. 1, Akro Agate to Fenton, Felt/Stoer	$24.95
6329	**Glass Tumblers**, 1860s to 1920s, Bredehoft	$29.95
5840	**Heisey Glass**, 1896 – 1957, Bredehoft	$24.95
6135	**North Carolina Art Pottery**, 1900 – 1960, James/Leftwich	$24.95
6335	Pictorial Guide to **Pottery & Porcelain Marks**, Lage	$29.95
5691	**Post86 Fiesta**, Identification & Value Guide, Racheter	$19.95
6037	**Rookwood Pottery**, Nicholson/Thomas	$24.95
6448	Standard Encyclopedia of **Carnival Glass**, 9th Ed., Edwards/Carwile	$29.95
5924	**Zanesville Stoneware** Company, Rans, Ralston & Russell	$24.95

DOLLS, FIGURES & TEDDY BEARS

6315	**American Character Dolls**, Izen	$24.95
6317	**Arranbee Dolls**, The Dolls That Sell on Sight, DeMillar/Brevik	$24.95
6319	**Barbie** Doll Fashion, Volume III, 1975 – 1979, Eames	$29.95
6022	The **Barbie** Doll Years, 5th Edition, Olds	$19.95
6221	**Barbie**, The First 30 Years, 2nd Edition, Deutsch	$24.95
6134	Ency. of Bisque **Nancy Ann** Storybook Dolls, 1936 – 1947, Pardee/Robertson	$29.95
6451	Collector's Ency. of **American Composition Dolls**, Vol. II, Mertz	$29.95
5904	Collector's Guide to **Celebrity Dolls**, Spurgeon	$24.95
5599	Collector's Guide to **Dolls of the 1960s and 1970s**, Sabulis	$24.95
6456	Collector's Guide to **Dolls of the 1960s and 1970s**, Vol. II, Sabulis	$24.95
6336	Collector's Guide to **Precious Moments Company Dolls**, Bomm	$19.95
6452	Contemporary American **Doll Artists** & Their Dolls, Witt	$29.95
6455	**Doll Values**, Antique to Modern, 7th Ed., DeFeo/Stover	$12.95
6465	**Madame Alexander** Collector's Dolls Price Guide #29, Crowsey	$14.95
5611	**Madame Alexander** Store Exclusives & Limited Editions, Crowsey	$24.95
5689	**Nippon Dolls** & Playthings, Van Patten/Lau	$29.95
5253	Story of **Barbie**, 2nd Ed., Westenhouser	$24.95
1513	**Teddy Bears & Steiff** Animals, Mandel	$9.95
4880	World of **Raggedy Ann** Collectibles, Avery	$24.95

JEWELRY, HATPINS, & PURSES

4850	Collectible **Costume Jewelry**, Simonds	$24.95
5675	Collectible **Silver Jewelry**, Rezazadeh	$24.95
3722	Collector's Ency. of **Compacts**, Carryalls & Face Powder Boxes, Mueller	$24.95
6468	Collector's Ency. of **Pendant & Pocket Watches**, 1500 – 1950, Bell	$24.95
4940	**Costume Jewelry**, A Practical Handbook & Value Guide, Rezazadeh	$24.95
5812	Fifty Years of Collectible Fashion **Jewelry**, 1925 – 1975, Baker	$24.95
6330	**Handkerchiefs**: A Collector's Guide, Guarnaccia/Guggenheim	$24.95
1424	**Hatpins** & Hatpin Holders, Baker	$9.95
5695	**Ladies' Vintage Accessories**, Bruton	$24.95
1181	100 Years of Collectible **Jewelry**, 1850 – 1950, Baker	$9.95
6232	**Plastic Jewelry** of the 20th Century, Baker	$24.95
6337	**Purse Masterpieces**, Schwartz	$29.95
6039	Signed Beauties of **Costume Jewelry**, Brown	$24.95
4850	Unsigned Beauties of **Costume Jewelry**, Brown	$24.95
5696	Vintage & Vogue Ladies' **Compacts**, 2nd Edition, Gerson	$29.95
5923	**Vintage Jewelry** for Investment & Casual Wear, Edeen	$24.95

FURNITURE

3716	**American Oak** Furniture, Book II, McNerney	$12.95
1118	**Antique Oak** Furniture, Hill	$7.95
3720	Collector's Encyclopedia of **American** Furniture, Vol. III, Swedberg	$24.95
6474	Collector's Guide to **Wallace Nutting Furniture**, Ivankovich	$19.95
5359	Early **American** Furniture, Obbard	$12.95
3906	**Heywood-Wakefield** Modern Furniture, Rouland	$18.95
6338	**Roycroft** Furniture & Collectibles, Koon	$24.95
1885	**Victorian** Furniture, Our American Heritage, McNerney	$9.95
3829	**Victorian** Furniture, Our American Heritage, Book II, McNerney	$9.95

ARTIFACTS, GUNS, KNIVES, TOOLS, PRIMITIVES

1868	Antique **Tools**, Our American Heritage, McNerney	$9.95
1426	**Arrowheads** & Projectile Points, Hothem	$7.95
6021	**Arrowheads** of the Central Great Plains, Fox	$19.95
5685	**Indian Artifacts** of the Midwest, Book IV, Hothem	$19.95
6130	**Indian Trade Relics**, Hothem	$29.95
6565	**Modern Guns**, Identification & Values, 15th Ed., Quertermous	$16.95
2164	**Primitives**, Our American Heritage, McNerney	$9.95
6031	Standard **Knife** Collector's Guide, 4th Ed., Ritchie & Stewart	$14.95

PAPER COLLECTIBLES & BOOKS

5902	**Boys' & Girls' Book** Series, Jones	$19.95
5153	Collector's Guide to **Children's Books**, Vol. II, Jones	$19.95
1441	Collector's Guide to **Post Cards**, Wood	$9.95
2081	Guide to Collecting **Cookbooks**, Allen	$14.95
6234	**Old Magazines**, Clear	$19.95
2080	Price Guide to **Cookbooks & Recipe Leaflets**, Dickinson	$9.95
3973	**Sheet Music** Reference & Price Guide, 2nd Ed., Guiheen/Pafik	$19.95

TOYS & MARBLES

2333	Antique & Collectible **Marbles**, 3rd Ed., Grist	$9.95
6548	**Breyer Animal** Collector's Guide, 4th Ed., Browell	$24.95
5681	Collector's Guide to **Lunchboxes**, White	$19.95
4945	**G-Men and FBI Toys**, Whitworth	$18.95
5593	Grist's Big Book of **Marbles**, 2nd Ed.	$24.95
3970	Grist's Machine-Made & Contemporary **Marbles**, 2nd Ed.	$9.95
6128	**Hot Wheels**, The Ultimate Redline Guide, 1968 – 1977, Clark/Wicker	$24.95
6466	**Matchbox Toys**, 4th Ed., 1947 to 2003, Johnson	$24.95
5830	**McDonald's** Collectibles, Henriques/DuVall	$24.95
6340	**Schroeder's** Collectible **Toys**, Antique to Modern Price Guide, 9th Ed	$17.95
6140	**Teddy Bear** Treasury, Vol. II, Yenke	$24.95
5908	**Toy Car** Collector's Guide, Johnson	$19.95

OTHER COLLECTIBLES

5814	Antique **Brass & Copper** Collectibles, Gaston	$24.95
1880	Antique **Iron**, McNerney	$9.95
6447	Antique **Quilts & Textiles**, Aug/Roy	$24.95
3872	Antique **Tins**, Dodge	$24.95
1128	**Bottle** Pricing Guide, 3rd Ed., Cleveland	$7.95
6345	**Business & Tax Guide** for Antiques & Collectibles, Kelly	$14.95
3718	Collectible **Aluminum**, Grist	$16.95
6342	Collectible **Soda Pop** Memorabilia, Summers	$24.95
5676	Collectible **Souvenir Spoons**, Book II, Bednersh	$29.95
5666	Collector's Encyclopedia of **Granite Ware**, Book II, Greguire	$29.95
5906	Collector's Guide to **Creek Chub Lures** & Collectibles, 2nd Ed., Smith	$29.95
3966	Collector's Guide to **Inkwells**, Identification & Values, Badders	$18.95
4864	Collector's Guide to **Wallace Nutting Pictures**, Ivankovich	$18.95
5929	Commercial **Fish Decoys**, Baron	$29.95
5683	**Fishing Lure Collectibles**, Vol. 1, Murphy/Edmisten	$29.95
6141	**Fishing Lure Collectibles**, Vol. 2, Murphy	$29.95
6328	**Flea Market Trader**, 14th Ed., Huxford	$9.95
6459	**Garage Sale** & Flea Market Annual, 12th Edition, Huxford	$19.95
3819	**General Store** Collectibles, Wilson	$24.95
2216	**Kitchen Antiques**, 1790–1940, McNerney	$14.95
5603	19th Century **Fishing Lures**, Carter	$29.95
6322	Pictorial Guide to **Christmas Ornaments** & Collectibles, Johnson	$29.95
5835	**Racing Collectibles**, Editors of Racing Collector's Magazine	$19.95
2026	**Railroad** Collectibles, 4th Ed., Baker	$14.95
5619	**Roy Rogers and Dale Evans** Toys & Memorabilia, Coyle	$24.95
3443	**Salt & Pepper Shakers** IV, Guarnaccia	$18.95
6570	**Schroeder's Antiques** Price Guide, 23rd Edition 2005	$14.95
5007	**Silverplated Flatware**, Revised 4th Edition, Hagan	$18.95
6239	**Star Wars** Super Collector's Wish Book, 2nd Ed., Carlton	$29.95
4877	**Vintage Bar Ware**, Visakay	$24.95
5925	The **Vintage Era of Golf Club** Collectibles, John	$29.95
6036	**Vintage Quilts**, Aug/Newman/Roy	$24.95
4935	The W.F. Cody **Buffalo Bill** Collector's Guide with Values, Wojtowicz	$24.95

This is only a partial listing of the books on antiques that are available from Collector Books. All books are well illustrated and contain current values. Most of these books are available from your local bookseller, antique dealer, or public library. If you are unable to locate certain titles in your area, you may order by mail from **COLLECTOR BOOKS**, P.O. Box 3009, Paducah, KY 42002-3009. Customers with Visa, Master Card, or Discover may phone in orders from 7:00 a.m. to 5:00 p.m. CT, Monday – Friday, toll free **1-800-626-5420**, or online at **www.collectorbooks.com**. Add $3.00 for postage for the first book ordered and 50¢ for each additional book. Include item number, title, and price when ordering. Allow 14 to 21 days for delivery.

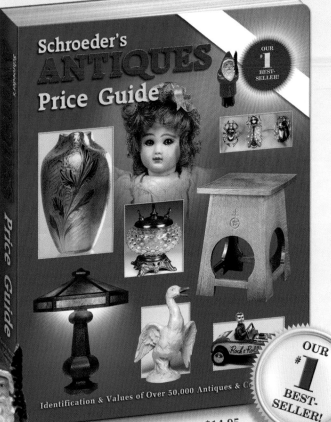